The Friendship
of Jesus and
God's Secret

The Friendship
of Jesus and
God's Secret

John Woolley

Winchester, UK
Washington, USA

JOHN HUNT PUBLISHING

First published by Circle Books, 2019
Circle Books is an imprint of John Hunt Publishing Ltd., No. 3 East St., Alresford,
Hampshire SO24 9EE, UK
office@jhpbooks.net
www.johnhuntpublishing.com
www.circle-books.com

For distributor details and how to order please visit the 'Ordering' section on our website.

Text copyright: John Woolley 2018

ISBN: 978 1 78904 093 7
978 1 78904 094 4 (ebook)
Library of Congress Control Number: 2018940517

A CIP catalogue record for this book is available from the British Library.

Design: Cecilia Perriard

UK: Printed and bound by CPI Group (UK) Ltd, Croydon, CR0 4YY
US: Printed and bound by Thomson-Shore, 7300 West Joy Road, Dexter, MI 48130

We operate a distinctive and ethical publishing philosophy in
all areas of our business, from our global network of authors to
production and worldwide distribution.

The Friendship of Jesus

Contents

Introduction

Jesus.

Just look at that name for a moment. It's magnetic, isn't it? If you're half-asleep, it wakes you up. If life has grown very dark for you, it seems to bring hope – even if it's only a flicker.

Jesus.

Keep looking at it for a second or two. In the whole world it's the one name which refuses to be ignored. Whatever your background or personality, you find you're *interested*.

People look at Jesus in trying to make sense of a world containing so many cruel contradictions.

- The refugee with those haunted eyes.
- The sad little black child, only hours away from dying.
- The young person in the next street lying ill with cancer.

It's not surprising that so many feel God doesn't exist – or that, if He does exist, He's just not interested in us. At the same time, you will find, everywhere, people who have a sort of instinct about Jesus. They're not completely sure about Him – but even just looking at His name they start to feel a bit more hopeful. There's a reason for this. Jesus is the only real hope of any person on this planet. (Big statement! We'll look at some of the reasons for it shortly.)

There's one thing absolutely certain: if anyone experiences the marvellous changes Jesus can make in a person's life, those arguments about whether He is divine become irrelevant!

If Jesus shares your life, you know beyond a shadow of a doubt that you've got God with you. You stop searching.

Is this you?

You may not remember when you were last inside a church – but you feel you'd like to know a lot more about Jesus. This book was written just for you.

Perhaps you are involved in a church – but are among the many who don't know Jesus in a warm and real way. This book was written just for you.

By the end of the book I have prayed that, whatever your age or personal makeup, you'll be well on the way to knowing Jesus – I mean really *know* him – as a friend. By the end of the book, I can almost hear you saying: 'I don't need a lot more reading or searching or wishing because I'm sure of Him!' This is because Jesus Himself will have been working in you – quite apart from your reading.

People in hospital were always asking me about Jesus (including many who were a bit frightened by organised religion!) – wanting to exchange that wishful longing for something better.

I wonder if you once had a strong faith – but you've almost lost it? I wonder if you have many problems in your life right now and feel that it's *His* help you really need?

Well, together, we'll look very closely at Jesus – this person who lived on earth at a definite time and place and is now in charge of everything we see around us. You will start the exciting process of getting acquainted with Him. You will find out how to *enjoy* that relationship – whatever your personality. Yes, *enjoy* – even if you're thinking right now how many huge barriers exist!

You've realised of course that discovering the friendship of Jesus doesn't all depend on you. In fact, He has already taken the initiative – giving you a wish to know Him. So, if you've all sorts of misgivings, all sorts of conflicts, all sorts of problems or if you're just among that huge number who can only say 'I wish …', here are two tremendous facts to get hold of:

- Jesus does want you to know Him. He doesn't play hide-and-seek with people.
- He does want you to *experience* how much He loves you.

Jesus wants to be, for you, not a cosy escape from life, but someone who is going to meet the hard realities of living with you. And this is going to make all the difference.

One to one!

There are always people frantically looking for an 'experience' of Jesus. Perhaps you too feel that He won't light up for you unless you find that dynamic service or inspiring meeting – as if He *needed* these occasions to break through.

You may be tempted to feel that, if you try a bit harder, read a few more books, He'll seem more real. Well, I've good news for you. You may not need to find the 'right' book or the 'right' Christian friend or the 'right' meeting.

There is one big step which so many people never get round to making. Will you take that step now – not worrying about the accompanying feelings as you do so!

Just ask Jesus (even if He seems rather remote at the time) to start sharing your life. He can't resist that request. Sharing your life is exactly what He'll start to do. You can forget looking for that spectacular 'experience'. Jesus is going to work His way – tailored just for you. You'll find that you're sharing all that He is – that you're part of Him. That isn't just fancy language, as you'll soon discover. Jesus will start to be real for you.

You'll find that you can feel calm, that you can feel strong by just having a word with Him. You'll find that a sense of Jesus with you throughout each day is not reserved for those few super-spiritual people!

On a hospital ward, a patient often said something like this to me: 'I'm not very religious, Padre, but, you know, I always think of Jesus as a friend.' Yes, there's that word again. He's a super friend! He's never beaten by any circumstances. He's completely dependable. You'll find that the true experience of Jesus, which is waiting for you, doesn't start off with a bang and then leave you disappointed.

To be realistic, you don't, of course, escape from all life's difficult places if Jesus is your friend. But you'll notice something wonderful. You'll notice Him making everything fit into a pattern for you – in a way which only God can do.

Yes, you too

Countless books have been written, haven't they? Many describe dramatic healings, lives being changed; all sorts of spectacular and inspiring incidents. I wonder if you're one of the majority who, after putting down the book, feeling very sad, has thought: 'That's great – but why doesn't it happen to me?' Well, from now on, you won't be one of those 'struggling Christians' who feel that knowing Jesus, in a warm sort of way, must be reserved for after you're dead!

Every category of persons needs Jesus – though some (like you) realise it more than others.

Here's Jane, aged 17. She was desperately shy and felt guilty about almost everything. She had to 'spoil' everything for herself. Jesus' love put things right, slowly but surely.

Here's Peter – a sad, elderly clergyman. He once believed very eagerly, but had only a dead feeling inside, after some events which left him disillusioned. Jesus 'came back' to put things right for Peter.

Here's Elizabeth, aged 42. She had prayed so desperately, for so long, but only occasionally felt close to God. Then Jesus gave Elizabeth a sense of His love – which changed everything.

By the way, we won't be spending a long time on admittedly important things like reading the Bible, attending Church and the various aspects of 'Christian doctrine'. These are dealt with by many others more expertly than I could do!

What we are going to do (and I suspect this is what you want) is:

- Start learning to be very *aware* of Jesus.
- Learn how to go through each day with a relaxing sense of His love.
- Learn how to start receiving His unique help for those, often desperate, needs and problems – things you may hide from those closest to you!

May I ask a favour? Forget about other people's spiritual 'success stories'. Forget all your previous disappointments – and look forward to experiencing Jesus sharing your life.

Your priority?

I think a pause would be useful right here, don't you? Could you, after a deep breath, promise yourself one thing? Promise yourself that knowing Jesus is going to be your top priority.

As you know, there was once the Great Train Robbery in Britain. One man – the head of the Flying Squad (Tommy Butler) – became obsessed with finding those responsible. He made countless trips abroad, missed many meals, went on hundreds of false leads – but never gave up. When he had just brought one more of the train robbers from the USA, a newspaper commented: 'Tommy Butler is the most dedicated cop in the business.' He had a ruling passion. He was in deadly earnest.

Shall I tell you something? The happiness of knowing Jesus as a Friend comes to those who put this *desire* for Him first – and keep it, in spite of perhaps years of disappointments. This is the way it happened for me – changing my whole life. And this is the way I'm sure it's going to happen for you.

But who is Jesus? It's natural to ask this, because so many who influence opinion in the Church, who appear on TV or who write books hold such frighteningly different beliefs about Him! So we'll take a look at Him now.

When working among hospital patients, I saw many prayers answered.

As a reader of this book, there has been a prayer said for you. It is that you will know, unmistakably, the companionship of Jesus – even if you've been at a 'wistful' stage for a long, long time!

I know that it's going to be a lasting friendship – long after you've finished the book.

Chapter 1

Who is Jesus?

'I can admire Him but ...'

'I suppose He's the greatest person who ever lived.'

'I can't believe all that the Bible says about Him, just because fairy tales are pleasant.'

Here you are in this vast, apparently impersonal, puzzling universe. If a voice whispered, 'Behind all this, I assure you, there is a loving God,' there are times when you might not be convinced!

'Believers' seem to fall, very roughly, into two categories. The first group put Jesus on a pedestal. He is God. He has all things in His hands. Watching Jesus walk about Palestine, people were looking at the God of this universe incredibly revealed in a human life.

Then there is a second group. While believing in God, they are not too sure about Jesus being all He claimed to be or was reported to be.

And so how does Jesus fit into the universe in which we say, 'There is a God who loves us', but which contains so much that is frightening or meaningless? For the honest person, the two seem so hard to reconcile, don't they?

Well, in this sort of world, don't you feel glad, as I do, that we've heard the name Jesus? You will have guessed that I'm not with those in the second group. I regard Jesus as supreme in the whole scheme of creation. Knowing what He has come to mean to me, and to so many that I used to meet in the wards of our hospitals, I couldn't do otherwise! In Jesus we experience all we will ever need to experience God. God the Father's tremendous love just shines through Jesus His Son – as much of that love as we could ever want.

They're one!

Using some cameras, you have to twiddle the knob until two images coincide. When they do, you're in focus. It's so sad that there are many people today who have two religious 'images'. First there's God, the Father, the Creator. Secondly there's Jesus whom they feel may or may not have been God revealed in human form.

It is when these images 'God' and 'Jesus' coincide, that religion starts to become excitingly alive! God, our Father, becomes real and close to you when you find Him in Jesus. Yes, I know it could be dangerous to confuse them, forgetting that there is a Father and there is a Son. *But both are God*. The real danger comes when they become 'split' – or when Jesus is slightly demoted, as so often happens today.

If you had a chance to eavesdrop on one or two people of deep faith saying their prayers, you'd find that the words 'Father' and 'Jesus' are used interchangeably towards the Person they are addressing.

Before those increasingly complex creeds were composed, the very early Christians seem to have had just one phrase by which they lived: 'Jesus is Lord'. For practical, working purposes, God was the God they saw in Jesus. Karl Barth, a giant among theologians, puts it in this way: 'From the very start, in trying to think of God, we've just got to think of Jesus Christ.' But many people today tend to push Jesus on one side with a big question mark over Him. And then they go on to say how sure they feel about God! It just doesn't work.

Jesus said to his friends in Palestine: 'If you've seen Me, you've seen God.' How about that! Think of what this means for you if you want Him to be your friend and companion. It's in Jesus that we see God *defined* in all His love and power.

Listen to an Indian doctor – bright blue turban, black beard – as he takes a few minutes off from the ward to ask about becoming a Christian: 'If you believe in God, what better way could

anyone imagine of Him revealing Himself than in a human life?'
Exactly, Dr Singh! You non-Christians are often more truly Christian than some of us 'professionals'!

He did it!

Have I perhaps been making it sound a bit too simple or a bit too patronizing? Because, after all, people have studied for centuries the complex question of just how the divine and human natures could meet in Jesus.

Well, even if the 'how' of it is rather puzzling, it is perfectly reasonable just to accept that God *did it* – that He showed us Himself, perfectly, in Jesus. If he didn't, I think I'd find it very difficult to believe in God in a universe like this, wouldn't you?

God, in fact, is not that unknowable 'wholly-other' being whom many sadly feel they have to accept. We look at Jesus and discover what a wonderful God we've got after all.

Rather like that little girl, blind from birth, who had the bandages removed after a successful operation, saw her father smiling down at her and said: 'Just to think I've had a lovely dad like that all along.'

So why not see yourself in Group Number One – ready to believe the very best of Jesus? If you do, the whole business of 'God' is going to come to life for you. I know that this is what Christianity is supposed to be all about – but sometimes you wonder what has happened!

The 'bigger' your view of Jesus, the more you're going to expect from Him. And with Jesus – just to show that He is God – you're not going to be disappointed.

It's always worth keeping firmly in mind that, when Jesus began life in that smelly stable, this was God breaking into our world and experiencing, in the closest possible way, all the hopes and all the heartbreaks of being human.

The New Testament, as you know, comes from a wide variety of writers – but you can't escape the message which runs right through: that Jesus is over all things – past, present and future.

Now, I realise that you will want to use your reason courageously. You won't want to hide from facts and create a fairy tale Jesus. But the remarkable thing is that countless people using the reasoning method about Jesus have ended up sure that He *is* someone on whom they can pin all their hopes.

You too can look forward to the time when all the arguments stop and there comes the certainty that Jesus is all that His loved ones through the centuries have said that He is.

I've been allowed to see Jesus do many wonderful things for people. But what I'm interested in now is Jesus doing something not for them, but for *you*.

Friend plus

Is 'Friend' just a sentimental and reassuring title, helping us to escape a little from the realities of life? Is it a pleasant fantasy which has nothing to do with what life is all about?

To have a true human friend is, of course, one of the most relaxing things. You don't have to pretend with that friend. That friend is concerned about you, shares with you, wants your best interests. But there will be many reading this who don't have a human friend in that category.

So what about the friendship of Jesus?

That friendship is all the things we've just thought about – but so much more. There's permanence (our loved ones or friends may be lost, of course); there's knowledge of our past, present and future – with a resultant wisdom which will always plan what is best for us. There is all the power and majesty of God.

I have the feeling that you're not going to give up now. If so, congratulations!

Dear Lord,
I'm aware of many doubts – about You and about myself. I can't
hide from You that often I'm unsure of Your existence. And yet I

feel that truly to know Your friendship is the best thing this life can offer. So please let me know You and, above everything else, as my Friend.
Thank you.

Chapter 2

Just Love!

People often forget that the friendship of Jesus really depends upon one thing. I'm sure you have guessed what it is. He doesn't become our Friend because of good works, our virtue, our church-going, our determination, the amount of *faith* we can produce.

You're ahead of me! You've already guessed what is the big factor. Yes, it all depends upon the *love* of Jesus. Let's think about it for a few moments.

There are those who come to feel the warmth of Jesus' love deeply. But, sadly, there are many others who, though they 'believe', do not feel His love for them at all. Many people have areas deep within where God is anything but love. At this deep level, there can be a feeling that He often treats His children worse than we treat our own. And so, although a person may outwardly protest, 'Of course, God is love,' it does always find an echo in the very deepest part of that person.

On this shaky foundation, many go on to build a life of trying to 'serve Him', 'helping the Church', which often becomes a grim business.

And so, task number one – and it's a pleasant one! Start thinking, as never before, about the indescribable love of Jesus, our Lord. See it in His life on earth. See it in the way He let Himself be killed for you and me. Look and look at that love – until it begins to sink deep into you.

And it does sink down, whatever those 'barriers' of yours. Deep inside you, God's Spirit is going to be working. And you'll become increasingly sure of Jesus' love for you.

Hold on a moment!

'Surely Christianity is not all about going around with a cosy sense of His love! What about the practical job of just doing what He tells us?' This is a down-to-earth member of the church down the road, who'll be popping up occasionally during the rest of our book – he's Adrian.

What Adrian is failing to realise is that those who really experience the love of Jesus every day *want* to please Him more than anything else.

In other words, 'doing what He tells us' coming naturally – rather than the grim (often resentful) 'obedience' and 'good works' of those who don't feel His love.

It's vital to allow *plenty of time* to think about the love of Jesus before 'finding His will' or asking 'what form shall my service for Him take?' So could we consider one or two things? They will sound pretty familiar, but it's surprising what can happen to you when you really focus on them:

- The love flowing from Jesus (which is the love of God our Father) just could not be stronger.
- The love is lasting love. He is not capricious.
- He *longs* for us to know that love.
- His dearest wish is our happiness.

I wonder if you are one of those who feel that they don't deserve His love? (A lot of people I talk to feel this way.) If you are, may I say:

- He, in fact, thinks the world of you – in spite of all you may think about yourself.
- He accepts you, with all your imperfections – which is why He is so much greater than often our consciences are!

People, in reaching out for God, have often been led to think, 'I must go and be useful for such-and-such a church,' and 'I must make some promises to Him.' They might have been wiser to spend a day or two just telling themselves *'He loves me!'* Though it appears that religion has been made very complex, it isn't really. It all hangs on those three little words.

So don't rush this vital stage of thinking about how much Jesus, our Lord, loves you. Don't be over-anxious for the moment, about what you feel you 'ought' to be doing for Him. Don't be anxious, even, about those personal needs with which you desperately want Him to deal!

Just let His love be very much in your thoughts. As you do so, the foundation is being built for His friendship to be experienced in increasingly exciting ways.

Dear Lord,
Please let me have a deep awareness of Your love – and let our friendship grow from this.
Thank you.

Chapter 3

What His Friendship Brings

Just a few moments to look at some things which happen if Jesus is your Friend. By the way, if you decide to seek *His* friendship, it's going to settle a lot of conflicts about smaller decisions in the future!

It means that you begin to give all your concerns from your often uncertain hands into His very sure ones. It means that, even when your situation is far from perfect, you're still going to enjoy Him with you.

Thinking of His love, you'll begin to relax a little. You'll begin to put your trust – not in your efforts, your 'status' or your achievements, but in what *He* is.

It will seem as if nothing in your life is outside Jesus any more. He will influence your thinking, conversations and decision-making. You'll be calm – and with a growing feeling that you're never alone. As the sense of the friendship deepens, you'll almost enjoy uncertain situations because you're meeting them with Him!

You're going to find that, instead of tense efforts at 'being virtuous', there'll be a new self – a Jesus-filled self. *How much a person misses, until he or she sees that living close to Jesus is much more about receiving and trusting than it is about trying frantically!*

Those situations, which used to send you to pieces – you're going to meet them successfully. You'll find yourself taking for granted that Jesus is in every situation before you reach it – and a wonderful thing happens. You become increasingly aware of 'adverse circumstances' actually being made to work for a good purpose – sometimes many times in a day. You'll find doors opening, things 'happening'; you'll find people coming (or not coming!). If Jesus really shares your life, He draws together all its complex interests and activities.

You?

I wonder if you're inclined to be shy, looking inwards a lot? With Jesus you begin to look away from yourself and your conflicts and increasingly at *Him*. This makes a huge difference in your life as you can guess. Ask some of those who used not to sleep very well! There's one tremendous thing about Jesus. He always helps us to believe in ourselves. And, because of this, you'll start to find a quiet joy of a sort you never had before – even at those times you used to call 'pleasure', even if you're hardly the dynamic or extrovert type!

Just a second to look at three people with whom Jesus was in contact:

- Zaccheus, tax collector, made a very undignified ascent of a tree to see Jesus.
- A woman with a long-standing illness pushed through a crowd, just to touch his clothes.
- A paralysed man, with friends' help, got himself to Jesus the hard way – through the roof.

They all 'meant business', didn't they? And, because of this, *something happened*. So don't forget that priority, will you?

I'm pretty sure that your wish is to deeply experience Jesus' friendship. If so, you can be sure about one thing – the process has *already begun*. And He's got so much to give you!

Dear Lord,
I may have misgivings, but I am going to expect the very best from you. Please help me, because I know you want me really to enjoy your friendship – always.
Thank you.

Chapter 4

Just Accepting!

This is probably the most difficult chapter in the book to write – because you're unique! It mustn't sound as if the friendship of Jesus depends on your going through some sort of formula. You don't have to find the right words, in order to 'capture' Him!

Jesus wants to grant your wish to know His love, in a way which will be indelible in your mind. He wants to do it in a way which will stand up to those swings of mood and sudden changes in your circumstances which lie ahead. So you've got to be pretty sure, on looking back, of what you thought and did at the time of really accepting His friendship.

You may have asked yourself the sort of questions which follow. They're worth asking, if you've never done so.

Here they are:

- Do I really want Jesus, not just as a helpful influence or because of some specific need or as a means of self-improvement – but as a friend who can do absolutely what He wants with me?
- Can He look at me and really know that He has all of me – ambitions, the future – everything? Can He?
- Am I prepared, not just to enjoy the comforting sense of His love, but to face some of the not-so-pleasant things in myself?
- Am I prepared to go with Him, perhaps through strange places, knowing that the only tragic thing in life is to walk alone – in the wrong directions?

When you consciously accept for yourself the love and friendship of Jesus, it's often accompanied by a desperate sense of 'needing something'. Sometimes too it's accompanied by a sort of abandonment – a throwing away of yourself, because you need Him so much.

Brian Hession was a brave man who inspired many who knew him by his wonderful faith, while under sentence of death and cancer. He once said that the most important step in the life of a Christian was the one in which he or she just 'went flop' in the presence of Jesus.

Yes, just dropping all our images, our pretences, and telling Him how very much we need Him. He loves to hear that!

I know you'll expect God to deal with each one of us in a distinctive way. Here's John – usually a confident, very self-sufficient person. He may be brought to a position of seeing how little he has without God or how much he needs the forgiveness of God. Here's Susan – she rather expects everything to happen fatalistically and passively. She may find Jesus leading her into letting herself influence events a bit more!

Be there!

You'd be surprised how helpful it is to find somewhere where you can be undisturbed and to think for a while about Jesus on the Cross. Just 'be there' in your imagination, at the greatest moment in all history. See them all – the soldiers, the sarcastic priests. In that moment Jesus saved a world which had cut itself off from God. Try reading the description of the Crucifixion in one of the Gospels, even if you think you know the story well. Try, for example, reading Luke's version – with no rush.

As you're thinking about all this, it's worth remembering that, because God transcends time, He already knew you and me during that event in Palestine!

Usually, as you look at the incredible love of Jesus on the Cross, you can't help making it very personal and realising 'He did that for me'. Did what? Well, He took *upon Himself* those callous and unloving ways I often find in myself. Jesus, so to speak, stood in the place of those alienated from God by their wrongdoing. His anguished cry of 'Why have you forsaken Me?' was His own sad experience of that separation.

There are some people who, when thinking about Jesus on the Cross even seem to hear Him gently speaking their name. No, it's not a morbid exercise! It's just a marvellous realisation of how much He loves His children. Whenever we look at the Cross in this way, it seems to make larger the place which Jesus has in our hearts. (It's something you'll probably be doing quite often, in the future.) Looking at the Cross can easily make a person say something like: 'I'm deeply sorry, Lord, for all that has been wrong.' By the way, this isn't to be labelled 'confession' as if part of a formula! It's something spontaneous when we really want to know His friendship. If our sorrow for all that has hurt Him is absolutely genuine and if there is a sincere wish to change for the better, forgiveness just pours out of Jesus, our Lord. We also find that His love helps us to forgive ourselves – not always easy for some! All this means that those days of feverishly trying are on the way out.

There's one request which Jesus finds irresistible. It's when we ask Him that we might learn to really love Him. Loving a supernatural being, of course, is hardly the easiest thing in the world! But I can assure you that it happens to every type of person you could imagine.

Loving Him so often grows out of *gratitude*. He's so patient with us in those early unsure stages. We just can't help being grateful – and love for Him just can't help growing.

When Jesus said, 'Ask and you'll receive,' it wasn't just to sound pleasant. *He meant what He said.*

Do you feel that you're not the type of person who could ever succeed in knowing Jesus' friendship? I know I did. But it happened. And it's starting to happen for you too. Don't rely on your words, but on His love. Be absolutely sure that, if you've asked Him to share your life, that request is granted. Life is going to be very different for you from now on.

Don't feel that the little prayer following is essential – as long as you know you want His friendship with all your heart. It is printed in case anyone would like to borrow a phrase which expresses what they want to say. I know He is going to bless you very much.

Dear Lord,
Here I am, with all my shortcomings, my fears, my current prob-
lems, my unfulfilled longings and dreams. Please take me and start
to make me what You want me to be. I am deeply sorry for all that
has been wrong in my life. Please forgive me. Please help my love
for you to grow – and, Lord, I gladly accept Your friendship now.
I thank You that there is going to be a growing awareness of Your
love – and that You will be exerting a good influence upon me all
the time. Lord, I am so pleased that you are my Friend – forever.
Thank You.

Chapter 5

Just Walking!

Someone once wrote a little verse about a bear cub who was very anxious about how to walk for the first time. He went on and on about this to his mother – should he put his right paw in front of the left or the other way round? Mother said, 'Don't talk – just walk!'

So here we are! Did you ask Jesus to share your life and be your friend always? If you did, should you be expecting to feel ecstatic? Well, most people aren't instantly ten feet off the ground at this stage. In fact you may not notice any dramatic change just yet. But hold on a moment – something is going to happen to you now. You're going to be steadier. You're going to be calmer. You're going to be more certain about Jesus and all that He is. And real joy is on the way. Or do you want to hear one more talented speaker? Perhaps – but this could start you off 'wanting' again – when that time has arrived, in fact, for you to start 'just walking' with Jesus as your Friend.

Just walking – knowing that *you now share all that Jesus is*. And, what's more, even in the early hesitant days you start living in heaven. This may sound a bit fanciful, but it's true. Jesus Himself showed us how it's done – although admittedly He's a rather exceptional example! In Palestine, as you know, His feet were very firmly on the ground. He wasn't playing a part, but experiencing all the limitations of being a human being. He wasn't dreamy or detached from life. He knew the real world with all its poverty. He mixed with people where life was cheap and life was cruel. But, because of His union with God the Father, His Body was on earth and His Spirit in heaven. It's a life of this kind which is offered to all who have Jesus as their friend. And you'll enjoy it more and more with each week that goes by!

Just walking. You want this friendship to be real. Well, nothing will make it more real than being absolutely honest. 'Lord, You do seem so remote at times' is *genuine* prayer.

Don't allow yourself even to slightly pretend or to say the 'right' things.

Honesty with Jesus is so relaxing. We usually want to be honest with someone who loves and understands us anyway. Such honesty begins to make Him feel wonderfully close. That 'Lord, You seem so remote' won't need to be said so often. As we talk to Him regularly, of course, the feeling that we're talking to ourselves begins to disappear.

Just walking, you'll start to 'look' at Jesus in a natural and effortless way. You'll become almost afraid to start on anything without a realisation (however brief) of Jesus with you. You're going to remember Him before every meeting and every conversation. Remembering that heavenly dimension to your life will become habitual.

You'll start giving that quick trusting glance to your Friend, even in the busiest, most absorbing situations.

This isn't to make Him 'do' things for you. What it does, though, is help you *keep an awareness* of His companionship.

As you start 'just walking', remind yourself, as often as you can, that Jesus is your Friend – for keeps. It may once have sounded too good to be true – but that is what has happened.

Your one fixed point through the rest of your life is this: *'I belong to Him'*.

Getting started

Well now, what about the average day? (If there is such a thing!) Aren't those earliest moments often make or break? One witty person commented that some people wake with 'Good morning, God!' and others, 'Good God ... morning!'

It's essential to give those very first moments to Jesus, your Friend. Many long-standing Christians fail to do this. In those earliest moments, as you know, your current anxieties and pre-occupations usually start to pop into your mind. Whether or not you're feeling very 'spiritual', this is the time to do two things:

- *Thank* Him for bringing you to the start of this day.
- *Give* the day to Him.

Just that, for the moment.

Of course, there will be those who are so tired of living that to face another day is something they would rather not do.

Giving the day to Jesus, our Lord, may seem a pretty formal habit, but in fact you can be absolutely sure that He is going to bless and use that day. He'll do it, even though we may be aware of still falling into the old ways.

For most people there is little time at the start of the day for 'being with' the Lord and telling Him what's in our hearts. But the thought of Him can nevertheless be there. It might be giving Him a two-second thought or whispering His Name as we go downstairs to switch on the kettle. This keeps us focused on *Him* in this early part of the day, which is so important.

This awareness of Jesus stops all sorts of upsetting or trivial thoughts rushing in and spoiling the mood of the whole day.

I'm sure you'll find a moment just to promise Him to try, with His help, to live in the way you know He would approve. Here's something which will help you:

Imaginatively meet the day with Jesus. 'See' yourself being calm, concerned about others you meet, not reacting with resentment, and so on. As we foresee the day with Him in this way, it increasingly works out the way we have previewed it. Allowing a few minutes for a quiet time, while caressing our mug of tea or coffee, is always well repaid.

Well, for most of us, that's it! There's breakfast, children to school perhaps, the rush to work. But there's no reason why Jesus should be very far from your thoughts. I know that you'll be watching for opportunities of breaking off, for a second or two, so that you can just 'be with' Him in those thoughts.

Dear Lord,
You know about my duties, and the people who may depend on me very much. Please show me opportunities in each day to just be quiet in Your presence.
Thank You.

Chapter 6

Just Thinking!

Those times when you can be alone with Jesus each day soon become times you just wouldn't miss. They're going to make such a difference to the quality of your day. These times should start *early* in the friendship, by the way – not something you learn after belonging to a church for ten years!

'Prayer' can be a frightening word – it is to some very active Christians! It takes so many forms, but there's one thing I hope you'll find time of, 'just thinking' about Jesus. We won't give this the grand title of Adoration or Contemplation. It's simply something we do which helps such a lot in deepening our awareness of His presence. It's even more helpful if there's no other aim than thinking about Him.

For example, perhaps you start thinking about how much Jesus loves you. It's natural to want to pass on from there to what else comes from being in His presence – His peace, His healing, His guidance, and so on. That's fine. Nothing wrong with that. And yet there will be times when just the thought of how much He loves you will be enough.

In other words, it will be enough simply to enjoy your Friend rather than some of the gifts or the much-needed 'results' of that friendship.

There'll be times, of course, when you're feeling very agitated – perhaps unable to sit down and think at all. More than anything, you'll want to be calm which the sense of His love brings. He understands perfectly our need of the things which flow from Him.

Don't have too many rules or 'patterns' – just as long as He is in your thoughts.

Let us say we've managed to steal two or three minuets apart with Jesus our Friend. It's a short time, but we find that He helps it to seem so calm and so unhurried. We can use a reflection along these lines – varying the words as we wish:

Lord, I think of all that You are ...
Your love:
Never changing
So very patient
So compassionate
Your wisdom:
the exactness of Your ways
Your perfect 'timing'
The way in which You can harmonise the circumstances of my life
Your greatness:
literally everything in Your control
nothing can happen which is not within Your will
only You can make difficult situations serve a good purpose.

However you may have been feeling when you started your time of quiet, you find that your reflection about Him brings a change for the better. It is this trust in all that He is which increasingly becomes part of our thinking. It spills over from the few minutes we spend with Him into the rest of our life.

Wasted time!

Remember Adrian? Our down-to-earth member of the local church is here again. 'Now look,' he says, 'is the friendship with Jesus all about sitting down and "drinking Him in"?'

No of course it isn't, Adrian. Most of our lives would not allow it anyway. But the daily walk with our Friend is very much about Jesus never being far from our thoughts.

Things have gone seriously wrong through great activity 'in His Name', but not very much thought given to Him! The greatest act of service for Jesus (so often neglected) is to give *Him our attention.*

People often ask what they should visualize at times of thinking about Jesus. You may have already worked this out. Some have in their minds their own image of our Lord as He was on earth; some glance at a favourite picture, just to stimulate their imagination; others merely visualize an 'aura of loving kindness'. It will vary from person to person anyway. The point is that imagination grows up into faith, so that we come to feel very close to Him – with or without our 'image'.

Is thinking about Jesus a cosy escape from reality – after which we're brought down to the real word – where people can be so difficult, our spiritual good resolves so easily shattered, things not working out as we planned?

It is precisely *because* people don't behave according to our expectations and because life *is* so complex, that we must let our Friend have as much of our thought as we possibly can. Time spent with Jesus always saves time. It saves time in fruitless effort, in bad relationships, in wrong decisions.

When you can create another few minutes to be alone with Him, here's a little reflection on what it means to *belong* to Jesus. Just lay aside all your concerns for a short time – and don't bother keeping rigidly to words used here, of course:

Lord, I do thank You that I'm Yours …
This means: I'm secure.
This means: I can be free of unnecessary burdens – because I'm Your responsibility.
This means: You can't fail me.
This means: I must do all in my power not to fail You.
This means: You are at work in me – all the time.
This means: I need not strive – even in spiritual things!
Thank You again.

If time is limited, you can always leave your time of reflection unfinished, to be returned to later. You may not get past 'secure' – but there's no hurry!

One very important thing which I'm sure you've realised: *times of thinking about Jesus are, of course, times when you are (consciously or unconsciously), absorbing what you see in Him.* We will think about this in a moment.

When on earth, our Lord was constantly misunderstood because of His consciousness of God the Father. The religious leaders diagnosed it as madness – or even worse. But Jesus never forgot the source of His life and His power. That is why He was the most perfectly balanced and really *sane* person we could ever find.

Jesus wants you to receive His life into your nature. He's going to be at work in such depth that you can't always distinguish between yourself and Him!

Jesus never wants to be just a helping agency. He wants to be our *life*. Now, this doesn't mean that we become mere ciphers, with our own personalities and talents disappearing. What Jesus, our Lord, does, in fact, is to make our real selves richer.

He shines through and enhances the good things He has already put into our natures. You're not John Brown cancelled out – but John Brown plus!

In our next chapter we're going to look at this process of 'absorbing' Jesus, our Friend.

Dear Lord,
It's exciting to think that I can share all that You are. I know that it will help me such a lot in the process of living in this very uncertain world.
Thank You.

Chapter 7

Just Absorbing!

Do you sometimes wish that you could change the present pattern of your life? Are you tempted to think that knowing Jesus would be so much easier in another environment, or another daily programme?

Well, I'm sure that you're beginning to realise that feeling closer to Him is possible in the most unlikely conditions. You may not need to run away from it all and become Brother Stephen or Sister Gillian!

If I were to ask each reader, 'How is the friendship of Jesus getting on?' I'd get some widely differing answers. This is because personalities vary so much (so did those of the first twelve of His disciples).

But, if you've been putting into practice some of the things you've been reading, I know that you *will* have started to have a stronger sense of Jesus with you. And, don't forget, there's no frantic rush. If your life is based on Jesus – talking with Him, sharing everything with Him, 'receiving' from Him – a lifetime won't seem long enough even to begin to perfect it.

Nothing in the world is more exciting than Jesus sharing His life with you. It's marvellous how changes are made in you not always by great efforts of willpower, but just by being in *contact* with Him.

Receiving from Jesus has been described in many ways: a wire receiving its electricity, a branch receiving from the main tree and so on. So you haven't got to ask Him, desperately, for this and that. All you have to do is receive what is *yours* anyway – because you're living with Him.

This process doesn't have to wait until everything in your life had been sorted out. You begin receiving and absorbing *now*.

Drawing closer

One warning: don't look fussily, at frequent intervals, to see 'progress'. As long as you keep this in mind, you're going to surprise yourself. You're going to start acting in ways which once seemed beyond you. Your reactions to situations will be improving. You'll find that you're fonder of people. Familiar things will give you more joy. You'll be more controlled.

Looking at Jesus:
Thinking of all that He *is*.
Thinking of all that it means to *belong* to Him.
Letting yourself *absorb* from Him.

If you're allowing these things to happen for the remainder of your life, you'll find that you're becoming closer and closer to Him and increasingly enjoying His company.

Can you manage to do something every day from now? Would you create a short time for thinking of how the qualities you see in Jesus really *are* becoming yours? You'll be really surprised what this does for you!

Try something like this:
Lord,
I think, gratefully, of all that I share, if You are my Friend:
Your peace: Thank You that it is growing in me.
Your patience: Thank You that this is growing too!
Your compassion: I share Your concern for others.
Your joy: It doesn't depend on circumstances!
Your strength: Thank You for a growing courage in areas where I used to be afraid.
Your wisdom: It is helping me to make fewer mistakes.
Lord, thank You that I am making increasing use of all that is mine
– united with You.

The best way to use that last little reflection is to *linger* over each of those qualities: 'Lord, I have peace ... Your patience'. No hurry – just letting His life sink in! As with the other suggested reflections you can easily break off in the middle if necessary and continue when you've a few more spare minutes later on.

Jesus. Go on receiving from Him (even if you can only manage a few two-minute occasions during each day). You'll always feel glad that you have that time apart with Him. And you'll find that this very elusive thing, peace, is growing in you. It doesn't make your personality completely impervious to changes of mood or to the effect people sometimes have on you. But you'll find that the sense of calm stays around for much longer periods than it used to – as long as you keep your eyes upon your Friend!

Dear Lord,
Thank You that I am beginning to receive into my nature all that You are. When, from time to time, I see progress, let me be thankful rather than complacent – knowing it's all due to You anyway. Thank You.

Chapter 8

Just Trusting!

Receiving all that Jesus has to share. It's a wonderful experience – especially if it happens within a life of complete trust in Him.

Complete trust? That's asking a lot! Let's see what's involved.

We usually give complete trust to a human friend, if there's a deep affection, don't we? But there exists the sad situation that so many followers of Jesus manage to give Him only *partial* trust. Their sense of depending on Him at every moment isn't always very strong!

It's not easy to trust someone we can't see. So what we usually do is to give Him varying amounts of trust – while trying so hard or so impatiently to shape events ourselves.

Not you again, Adrian! Go on then: 'Well, look – does all this mean that, if Jesus is our Friend, we can just sit back and do nothing to influence the details of our lives?' No, of course not, Adrian. It does mean, though, really allowing Him to work (which so many of you 'busy' Christians fail to do).

So often a person will say, 'Oh yes – all things are in His hands,' and then go on to plan so furiously and to make so many moves (not always very successfully).

Have you ever said a prayer about a difficult situation, which has then shown absolutely no improvement? Have you had to ask yourself, 'Is God really in control? Is he influencing this situation or not?'

It's as if you're challenged either to trust Him completely or not at all. Not easy, is it? When things are bad, there's often a terrific pressure on us to give up trusting.

There's a conflict: 'This trust is getting me nowhere fast ... or perhaps I really *should* give Him a chance.' And so ... there may be a few hasty phone calls – or there may not!

What about ways of developing complete trust in Jesus?

One sure way is to think often about how *great* He is. Nothing is outside His control. Every possible combination of circumstances in your life He can shape.

As you do this, you soon find yourself quietly saying (in the most chaotic situations) 'It's in *Your* hands, Lord.'

You'll soon grow towards complete trust if you keep the concept of *Friend* very much in your mind. It's not simply that He chooses not to fail you – His friendship is such that He *can't*!

Remember this when things seem to be getting worse instead of better or answers to your desperate prayers seem delayed. Yes I know it's hard, but keep holding on to Jesus. He's not going to allow anything which, in the long term, could be disastrous for you.

Something else to remember is that He trusts you! He's not blind, of course, to your imperfections and many mistakes. And yet, those who follow Him soon get this feeling – that He trusts *them*. It's as if He were looking at you and saying, 'I know you can do it!'

Real trust

How else is real trust developed? You may have discovered already that it develops in life's frightening places and in those shattering reverses. I meet so many people who, realising there was literally no one who could really help, had to just throw themselves upon God.

When they did so, they found how loving, how patient and how much in control He was. And now they've a trust which no one can break!

The ingredients of a 'trust situation' between Jesus and yourself are:

- His greatness.
- Your patience.

That second one is hard, isn't it? So often we're not aware of how He *is* at work – providing for us, working out complex situations for us. Later, though, we can see just what He's been doing.

Over and over again you'll be able to look back upon a pattern of events involving individuals, choices, chance meetings – which all combined to give the desired result. Every day, I'm amazed at the way He influences very difficult situations (or rather I've stopped being amazed because He does it so often).

Because of His great love for you, Jesus, our Lord, will always *anticipate* what you need. He's already preparing what is required in your case. One verse in the Bible puts it very well: 'Before they call, I will answer!'

Another thing we learn as we start growing towards complete trust in Jesus is His *timing*. A course of action may seem right. A situation may seem greatly to be desired – but it has to be in His way, and in His time, to be most effective.

Adrian is bursting to come in: 'Surely, when a thing seems right, we have to do something; surely there are times when a choice has to be made pretty quickly? We can't just "leave it all to the Lord".'

Agreed, Adrian. There are many times when prompt action is called for. As long as there's a sense of His friendship, giving you an awareness of *when* to act decisively!

Let's suppose you've prayed about a situation and a course of action seems both right and urgent. You can go ahead! But commit your actions and its consequences to Him. And then bring Him into each developing pattern of circumstances. You must be prepared for Him to say, 'That's enough for the moment,' and accept it, when you're aware He is checking you. (*Events* often show us how He's allowing some things, but not others.)

Real patience is not the easiest thing to acquire, is it? But, if you're beginning to live close to Jesus, you're absorbing His patience, which should encourage you.

You'll find that Jesus is a Friend who deserves your *complete* trust at every stage of your life. I know that you're going to give Him this trust.

There will be many times when you'll look at the way things have been happening and tell yourself how glad you are that you banked upon Him!

Dear Lord,
I realise that a growing trust is what following You is all about.
Help me to develop the patience and the flexibility of one who knows
You are constantly at work on my behalf.
Thank You.

Another pause!

Having been reading about (and practising I hope!) things like reflecting, absorbing, trusting, you've earned a breathing space.

As you look back on our book so far, you'll have noticed how often Jesus' *love* has been mentioned. This hasn't been to give a nice 'tone' to the book. Far from it. It's been mentioned so many times for a definite reason. It's because being aware of His love is the key to lots of areas which people find very, very difficult.

Being conscious of His love is the *decisive* factor in almost anything you can think of. Things like:

- How you see the people around you – and the influences you have upon them.
- Your standards of behaviour – and how far you manage to live up to them!
- A *true* view of yourself.
- Answered prayers.
- A deep joy, contrasting with that 'brightness' which some Christians turn on – and which makes you want to run a mile!
- A real desire to please Jesus.

This awareness of His love finds its way into everything which can possibly happen to you on this planet.

There is still no need to hurry your reading. Go on thinking about His love. Allow plenty of time for experiment in real-life situations, based on what we've covered so far.

If you're making time for 'being with' Jesus your Friend, you can be sure that His love will become stronger than anything else in your experience. It will become the answer to everything.

And He's working, all the time, to bring you into a deeper relationship with Himself. Don't be one of those Christians who doesn't *allow* Him to work!

Chapter 9

Secret Place

David is brought into hospital for the last few days of his life. He is in the terminal stages of a disease – and special drugs are ordered to help him.

David has always trusted Jesus. When the chaplain goes to see him, it's David who says the prayer – for them both!

We watch him getting weaker – and still showing no concern about his situation. He seems to be *'somewhere else'* other than in the ward. No, he's not confused or drowsy – in fact very alert. The only way to describe it is that he is *protected*.

Eventually he dies. Then we learn that the drugs were never used. The nursing staff are amazed. David, with all sorts of un-dignified and uncomfortable things happening to his body, has been in what is sometimes called God's secret place. This is not a romantic creation of the imagination; it's a place very real to those who know Jesus as a Friend. As your trust in Jesus grows, I know that you'll increasingly use this place – *known just to you and Him.*

Many people who would never dream of calling it 'God's se-cret place' use it just the same! They instinctively go there when life becomes frightening or uncertain. It's not an escape from reality, by the way, because Jesus usually makes you more aware of the hard facts of life.

You've probably found that getting away from it all is nev-er quite enough. It's hard to run away from yourself and your fears, isn't it? But in this place, in which the occupants are Je-sus and yourself, you can start to relax a little, however difficult things are. You relax in what *He* is.

This secret place, shared with Jesus, becomes increasingly real as we make use of it. It can be used when alone in the mountains, it can be used when jostling around a supermarket. It's not just somewhere for times of crisis, but a place we get used to being in at *any time*. It doesn't matter how you personally visualize it or what you call it, as long as you use it.

People often feel threatened, not only by influences from the world outside, but by things from their own minds. Not always easy to distinguish between the two sources! *But the answer is the same in each case.* Jesus is able to act as a protective shield in that deepest part of our being – our spirit. He protects that deepest part of us even from some of the strange things our mental processes get up to.

I sometimes suggest to those who feel under pressure from a variety of frightening and negative thoughts to picture Jesus coming between them and these things. I'm often told later how well this has worked. It works because they're not engaging in a naïve exercise in auto-suggestion (which might horrify a self-respecting psychiatrist), but because Jesus is *actually doing* what they are trusting Him to do.

You probably know how it feels to have everything under control spiritually – prayers seem easier, sailing through temptations, God feeling closer. Then … crash! There's a devastating crisis. Can we deal with it or will it break us down completely?

However bad a person's situation (and yours could be pretty difficult right now), it's vital just to 'be with' Jesus in this place in His love. And then, through the reminder of the crisis, however long it may last, to continue there while He works – both in the situation and in you. You may have given that set of circumstances to Him mechanically at first, with very little hope. But increasingly the fact that He's in it with you is going to make all the difference. Being in a place shared just by Jesus, by the way, doesn't affect the way in which we share experiences with loved ones and others. What happens is that, as we use this secret place, we become very different people in the way we *react* to life. We learn to keep the disturbing things outside His love.

Dear Lord

Help me make increasing use of your secret place. Let me stay so close to You that to be anywhere else seems unusual! From the place which I share with You let me offer help to those who may themselves be passing through a very difficult time.

Thank You.

Chapter 10

Just Sharing!

Even as you're getting to know Jesus better, it sometimes happens that at the end of the day you have to admit something like this: 'I'm sure I haven't really helped anybody today. And as for being filled with joy and power ... well!'

In other words, the day contained a lot which couldn't be put into the category either of truly giving or truly receiving.

Let's risk annoying Adrian by one of those apparent over-simplifications: *Living with Jesus is all about being conscious of His love – and sharing it.*

'Now just a moment,' says Adrian, quick as a flash. 'Surely no one achieves a life filled with blissful meditation, going round giving out the love of Jesus to everyone in sight. Isn't it a little bit removed from reality?'

Well, Adrian, for many 'struggling Christians' it may seem just an ideal. But the fact is that He wants us to fill our lives with as much as possible of *two things*: Ready?

- *Receiving* from Him (about which we've said quite a lot already).
- *Giving* (letting Him touch or speak to others through us).

Sometimes a false contrast is made by Adrian and his friends. They see two groups of people: those living a life of prayer and meditation and the others who 'get things done'. You won't be taken in by this sort of thinking, I'm sure.

The only place from which you'll really begin to help others bring some positive change in their lives is, in fact, the place where you are conscious of Jesus' love. This doesn't mean, by the way, that, when you're with other people, you're trying, dreamily, to keep a sense of Jesus with you (more about this in a moment).

We find that time we've spent thinking about and talking with Jesus has not been a cosy, escapist indulgence, but an absolute necessity. From this place in His love the greatest and most exciting thing we can do in this life starts to happen: our meetings with others and our prayers for them, bringing the unique help of Jesus Himself!

Marvellous things happen when we're living close to Jesus. A hospital chaplain, for instance, soon learns that his own personality and the things he says or does at the patient's bedside are not the things which really change the patient's situation (even though God does, of course, use our personalities and gifts). What really works is *keeping close* (i.e. being sure He's often in our thoughts). He said, 'Without me, you can do nothing.' In other words, 'It's what I do, when you're united with Me, that's going to *last*.'

In His way

First of all, then, don't rely only on your reason, your carful planning or your bursts of enthusiasm in setting out to 'share' Jesus your Friend. It's far, far better just to be surrendered to Him, prepared to be very flexible in the way He uses you. Otherwise there may be great activity in a certain direction, with very little achieved!

Just a word spoken to someone as we live close to Jesus, ready to be used as *He* wishes, can change that person's situation more than many thoughtfully planned schemes. *Jesus* is in that word!

Never forget that what each follower of Jesus can give to others is going to be very different. You may be able to tear round the wards of a hospital, but you could, instead, be confined to a wheelchair and only 'share' Him with one other person during an entire week. It doesn't matter! He only wants you to promise Him that, as far as possible, the lives (even if only one or two) which touch yours will be made even brighter.

We never have to look round (once we've made that promise) for people to help. He confronts us with them! And often they're people close to us, whose needs we've never noticed before.

Remember that, even while you're still 'only growing' in a sense of Jesus' friendship, He'll be using you. Even while you feel how inadequate you are, He'll be using you. Just as long as you've put yourself at His disposal!

Just what is it that Jesus does which is so much more effective than our eloquence, good intentions, strategy? Well, it's not merely that Jesus in you makes you a shining *example* to the world. Something else is happening. There's a very definite *influence* from Him – through you.

Christians often forget that not only is He 'with us' but with us to be *used*. He longs to be, through us, a dynamic influence. In any situation where Jesus is *allowed to work*, this influence exists. I'm always seeing very agitated people suddenly become calm and start to talk hopefully – not through any words of mine, but because Jesus is there with us!

Here's something you might like to do (if you've not done it so far) about contacts you have with people. Ask Jesus, our Lord, to help you to see them through *His* eyes of love – and He *will*. Then thank Jesus, in sheer trust, that *something is happening* between Him and the person you're with.

A doctor, nurse, minister, social worker or anyone in frequent contact with broken-hearted, frightened people can't ask God for any better gift than that of love. It's *His* love with which we now love others – our own may be a bit selective or unpredictable! And so you, in your own unique circumstances and with your own unique opportunities, are always wise to ask first for His love to be in you. We know, don't we, how often a mum literally 'loves' her child better?

Mr A who *loves* is going to help someone more than even Mr B, that prominent charismatic figure, of powerful faith, praying equally powerfully!

Being conscious of Jesus, by the way, doesn't mean that you're performing mental gymnastics. You're not trying to concentrate upon a friend and, at the same time, straining to contemplate *Him*. (Your acquaintance would rightly be annoyed if he knew.) It simply means that the other person gets your full and loving attention, but, at the same time, never far away, there is an awareness of just whose Presence you are in. One of the many things which Jesus our Lord does so well is helping us to be aware of Him – *without anything less going to the other person.*

He's in it

What you've tried to share with someone may seem a bit trivial. It may be a smile or a quick, reassuring comment. But He will be in it.

So thank Him from time to time from what He did in your encounters with other people, even if you're not always conscious of just what He *did* do!

A smile has often stopped a potential suicide and that reassuring remark of yours (especially if Jesus is part of it) can go right through a darkness which you never dreamed existed.

Have you been thinking that 'Jesus reaching others through us' isn't quite the whole story? You're right. When we act lovingly towards people, *He* receives too – that's how closely He is identified with us. I know that it's a bit hard to visualize, but never forget how much He is *involved* in that interaction of human beings – involved in both the 'giving' and 'receiving' capacities! That's why we must never feel smug in our private relationship with Him and perhaps be acting coldly, or deprivingly, to someone close to us – not realising that we're hurting Him too.

There's always a temptation to forget that Jesus not only works through you but *for* you. He really is helping those you say a prayer for – often without your contact with them. And He completes (in a perfect way) those imperfect 'practical' things you attempt for Him.

By the way, although Jesus wants to be able to depend on you in the important things each day, He wants you also to enjoy His gifts and His world! Many very kind Christian people, including some clergy and ministers, temporarily forget this and then break down completely. He's not merely a Friend whose company we can learn to enjoy – He enjoys *ours*. And so you are 'doing something' for Him when you take time just to be with Him, to enjoy Him and enjoy His creation.

Life can't be boring when you know that Jesus is at *work* through you. He lifts your encounters with others into a completely new dimension.

Because He's sharing life with you, you can be absolutely sure that no time you spend with someone else is being wasted.

Dear Lord,
I would like Your love to flow, more and more, to everyone I meet.
May what I say or do, each visit I make, each letter I write, each prayer I say make a difference to someone's life.
Thank You.

Chapter 11

When It All Goes Wrong

Say something nice to everyone you meet today – it'll drive 'em crazy'.

So say one of those colourful posters with which youngsters often adorn their bedroom doors.

It reminds us, of course, that our best intentions can so easily fail.

Everything getting streamlined in living close to Jesus and then – crash! We find we've hurt someone or we've scored a great miss somewhere. 'Your religion doesn't do much for you,' says an acquaintance and bump we go.

The pressures on those who share life with Jesus and look like being useful to Him can be subtle. Many occur in that tricky sphere, relationships (e.g. within families).

Things like pride, anger, lack of patience, crop up just here, don't they?

There's no more difficult part of life than that of getting along with others – including, of course, those closest to us!

Factors influencing our relationships are, as you know, complex. There can be clashes of basic temperament, ignorance of our own and others' behaviour motivations, two people pursuing entirely different objectives and other influences which we can't always detect.

Is advice enough?

Let's say that twelve writers set out what they saw as important about living with other people.

Provided that you could endure all this advice, you'd be awfully confused by the end of it and probably feel like banging your head against a convenient wall.

The writers would probably cover self-evident things like the need for patience, putting others at ease, not manipulating or exploiting others, trying to see another's viewpoint, jumping on pride, being more ready to listen, acting lovingly when not feeling inclined to do so – and so on.

Those writers knowing some psychology would step in with insights into the motivations of your actions, help in understanding people more deeply (so that you aren't constantly angry or disappointed in your expectations of them) and help in understanding yourself and the unconscious pressures upon you.

I'm sure you'd find it all helpful in avoiding many mistakes and yet there'd be something missing, wouldn't there? *Failures would still be happening in relationships!* You'd feel like saying, as that honest man Paul did: 'I don't do what I want, but instead keep doing the things I hate.' Today Paul might have said: 'Here I am, mentally equipped by ethical and psychological teaching, to make a real success of living – but I keep putting my foot in it!'

You'd get very discouraged if it wasn't for that thing we thought about earlier – the *influence* of Jesus. Make sure that your encounters with people are under this influence (which they are if He's in your thoughts a lot). Jesus has a wonderful way of neutralizing 'contra-influences' and incompatibilities.

Talking of 'contra-influences', many believe, of course, that it's not just chemical makeup or earliest experiences that affect our relationships. In addition to God's influence (producing reasonableness, unselfishness, patience) there is the influence of supernatural evil, (seeking to produce mistrust, resentment, intolerance and even, of course, murderous anger).

I know that in some places today it's not fashionable to think this way! But Jesus, our Lord, was very sure about this pressure on us by evil, wasn't He? And because He saw it for what it was (because He made the right diagnosis) He had a unique success rate in making people happy and well again, didn't He? But never mind for the moment the true source of negative influences. The vital thing to remember is that *God has the answer to them.*

By the way, don't get like Mr A who blames supernatural evil for *everything* that goes wrong instead of taking responsibility himself. Involved in a stormy relationship, Mr A soothes himself with the thought: 'This is all happening because I'm a good Christian and the other people aren't.'

Well, of course, it's true that, if you follow Jesus, it's going to arouse antagonism. He warned us that it would. There are times when you're disliked or misunderstood for trying to do God's will – and only kept going by the thought that at least *He* understands.

But it's dangerous to go on to assume that people's hostility is always aroused by our goodness.

Disharmony! Could you possibly be in such a state with someone right now? At least you know how it feels. One disharmony can darken the whole of your life, can't it?

And a hurt-feeling situation occurs so unexpectedly, doesn't it? Often there's no immediate opportunity to 'put things right'.

The *only* thing we can do is to bring this to Jesus our Friend until such an opportunity comes. We bring to Him the other person – and the situation.

You won't be surprised, of course (especially if you've tried it) that this works wonderfully. I've seen so many people 'made friends' (much better than they were previously) because someone *prayed*. It's just as well that we don't always get that opportunity to 'sort it out' with the other person in our own way! It's part of our Friend being *allowed* to exert His influence – being given space in which to work! The old advice about getting out of a room and praying, before a quarrel gets worse, is very sound.

Does what I've just said sound a little too good to be true? It would be wrong to pretend that you *always* see immediate results, but patience and trusting restraint work wonders. You'll find that 'bringing Jesus in', as an automatic action, works miraculously in dealing with hurts and misunderstandings.

Resentments! Christians will quickly agree that it's 'harmful to have them' but, oh dear, how often, when we talk to a Christian, we find a *huge* resentment lurking!

Here's something you can do if there's a resentment lurking in you. Ready? Look at the resentment-causing situation with your intellect rather than with your emotions – as if you were an interested third party! Give the resentments to Jesus, your Friend. Let His love in you dissolve it. Ask Him to do what you may find it hard to do. Ask Him to bless the other person. Yes, you'll find that you really do want something good to happen to Mr B who treated you so badly! A relationship is on the way to being mended – with someone living or dead.

By the way, hurts and resentments can largely be prevented from ever intruding in the first place. What you do is to mentally 'set people free' (you no longer demand nor expect from them gratitude, praise, recognition or their supposed 'duty' towards you).

When things go wrong, have you tried 'seeing' the other person and yourself, together, in the light of God's love? See other influences excluded (and then *hold* to that picture). You'll usually see improvements. These are sometimes dramatic, sometimes gradual – we're not always aware of why some take longer than others!

Bringing Jesus into every relationship and allowing Him to work isn't some 'way-out' form of Christianity. It's *normal* Christianity in one of its very neglected aspects.

It's no wonder that so many 'believers' don't feel Him very close when they leave Him out of things so much.

You wouldn't want a long and very obvious list of those temptations and 'pressures', which can cause any day to go wrong. And so the only one I'll mention is spiritual pride – because it's the most sinister! The big danger is to see ourselves as 'super-Christians' compared with others and to forget that all our 'progress' is due to God anyway. Fortunately He often lets

us see ourselves entering this state: 'There I go again, Lord – I'm
sorry. Knock this out of me for good.'

You'll win!

Just as temptations and pressures differ widely, so will the ways
you personally find helpful in overcoming them. What often
happens is that, through habit, you're caught off guard and find
you've already begun a wrong pattern of thinking or conversations. Never mind! Just glance to Jesus and *refuse the deliberate
continuation* of that pattern. And so the next comment to your
companion at the breakfast table could be one of compliment
rather than criticism! With Jesus it works. Try it.

By the way, don't forget the value of the *pause* when under
pressure to commit yourself to some wrong word or action. St
Paul called it the way of escape. The longer the pause (taking a
good look at Jesus as we do) the weaker becomes the pressure
on us. The feeling of being united with Jesus is marvellous in
sailing through those things which used to knock you for six.

Lord,
*I realise that people won't always behave in the way I expect – of-
ten I'll be disappointed in them. And, often, I'll be disappointed in
myself! Help me to use You, in every kind of pressure which would
deflect me from the way which pleases You.*
*I'll remember to bring You in – straight away – when everything
goes terribly wrong.*

Love – all the time

Would you like to acquire a habit which will change, dramati-
cally, the way you live? You would? Well, start to think about
Jesus' love as *surrounding* all that you do. See everything (alone
or with others) as happening in the context of that love – a way
of thinking which will become automatic.

Here's a list you can go through in His presence whenever

there's an opportunity (take your time over it).

Dear Lord,
I remind myself of all that results from consciously living in Your love:
In Your love, I need not fear anything – nor need I ever act out of fear.
In Your love, I'm able to keep a quiet joy – even when everything is difficult or threatening.
In Your love, my love for You keeps growing.
In Your love I'm learning serenity and I'm not 'trying' so frantically!
In Your love, I'm instinctively refusing what I know would hurt that love.
In Your love, there's a healing influence upon every part of me.
In Your love, Your work of drawing me closer to Yourself goes on continuously.

Thank You. In Your love, I'm learning.

Chapter 12

Just Reflecting!

'I wish I could be more like Jesus,' sighed a young man who had recently taken a revealing look at himself.

Well, he needn't worry, because in a world of increasing specialisation there's one very difficult skill possessed by Jesus, our Friend. It's that of changing *people*.

Do you know the best thing that anyone can ever think about you? It's that they can see *Jesus* in you. But it's better, of course, if they don't tell you! Don't listen to Adrian or anyone who claims that there isn't any 'Christian activity' more important than reflecting Jesus. If you're reflecting Him, it won't make you say: 'I've made great progress in being virtuous.' But it will make an agnostic friend think: 'There's something in Christianity after all!'

And so, how does it all start – the exciting process of Jesus changing us, so that *He* is reflected in us?

Well, you've found already that being aware of His love makes you genuinely sorry about anything in your life which may be hurting Him. It makes you want, desperately, to do better. You develop a 'being sorry' potential. Does this sound a bit morbid? It isn't really.

What Jesus does is to give you *realism*. You'll see progress – OK! But you'll see one or two things urgently needing to be put right. A few not-so-good tendencies could have crept in lately alongside those 'spiritual advances'!

The ideal starting point in the change process is when we start to say: 'Lord, make me aware of anything so habitual that I never dream it's hurting You.' A lot of long-established Christians could do with asking this!

Yes – a new person!

Have you noticed something about the list which Jesus gave of the happy people? There were, of course, the peacemakers, the merciful, the humble-minded.

But there's one group different from the rest. It's this: 'Happy are those who are hungry and thirsty for goodness'. Aren't you glad He found room for it? No 'attainment' mentioned – it's just the *wish* to change which He sees as a virtue in itself!

So how about this wish being *your* steady intentions? He sees it when you only see your failures.

Don't forget:

- The *wish* to be someone Jesus is pleased with.
- Forgetting about the process, as far as possible. (He will allow you glimpses of your progress, so do not worry.)

He'll be making you into a *new* person, even if you're looking in vain for changes right now!

Here's something to realise. While you've been thinking about Jesus, letting Him work in you, many things about you have been changing. You probably think that most things haven't altered. But there's one basic test: do I want to please Him now, where once I wanted to please myself? Do I? Do I?

Is the thoughtful answer 'Yes'? If so, He's definitely creating a new person in your case!

Here is something which will help along the change process. Say to Him at odd times during each day, 'Lord, just what *You* want' (or words to the same effect). Smile when you do so! Don't have a grim stoical 'acceptance' – as if what He wants for you must be something awful!

This will put you on to a sort of 'obedience wavelength' – doing the right things without even thinking about them.

'A lot of talk about Jesus changing us. What about *our* effort?' (Yes, Adrian again.)

Well, I often find things happening (after bringing to Him problem situations) where I haven't done a thing – except tell Him about it! But our Adrian has a point. Jesus does look for *our* effort in many cases and then influences that effort towards success.

Do you think He might be looking for an effort from you in giving up one or two things which are preventing you from really enjoying Him?

Don't forget that, in place of what goes, He'll always give you something far, far better.

Have you been thinking, 'What about those times when I want to act like a new person, but find a tremendous pressure in the opposite direction?'

There's only one thing to do at such times. Very deliberately look at your Friend, Jesus, to literally *take you through* the making of that choice. It often involves an effort – but He'll always complete your effort successfully.

The more closely united you are with Jesus, the more aware you'll be of the way to take a tricky decision – provided you're doing what pleases Him in those other things where the right course *is* clear.

It's happening

Jesus said He wanted you to be a light in this confusing world. He didn't mean that you were to perform certain duties, very self-consciously, hoping other people would see Him in you! He just wants you to let Him live and work through you, so that His light is automatically reflected – with you probably unaware of it.

Don't get worried if you start noticing even more differences between Jesus and you. That's progress. Keep looking in His direction rather that at yourself to 'see' changes. You'll soon know that things are happening – you'll be saying, 'Yes, I *know* I'm calmer. I *know* I'm more controlled. I *know* I'm more at ease with people. I *know* I'm not upset by the things which used to upset me.'

By the way, don't throw away (in a careless moment or under temporary pressure) gains you've made. Going back to square one can usually be avoided, with just a little more firmness, and His help guaranteed!

Climbers who have negotiated dizzy ice-walls with experienced guides have described a definite feeling about those leading them. It's a deep sense of companionship – and it is all produced by carrying out their guide's directions!

If you want to reflect Jesus, He makes you a promise (you'll find it in John's Gospel). He says that, if you let Him lead you and change your reactions, you'll start to 'live in His love'. In other words, you'll not only be changing – but you'll have a strong sense of His companionship.

'Special offers' are tempting, aren't they? Jesus makes a marvellous one: 'Accept a fairly easy "burden" (that of pleasing Me), and I'll let you unload on to Me your often huge burdens and problems.' In other words: 'Just carry out My wishes and leave Me to handle yours.'

It isn't just strong and confident people who 'arrive' at living harmoniously with Jesus and at reflecting Him. Success also comes to those who battle along very unsurely, very apologetically and with lots of failures. You?

Jesus never goes on strike when you fail. He doesn't get discouraged and give up, provided you go on *wanting* to be more like Him. He'll always pick you up after failures. He'll take you on to levels where your wishes harmonise with His – and *His* reflection in you gets brighter and brighter!

Dear Lord,
I know I can trust You to make me the sort of person who reflects
You. If there is lurking in me any area of reluctance to change,
please help me to deal with it.
Thank you.

Chapter 13

Fact-Based Prayer

Imagine that you possess a listening device and overheard the prayer of someone who tries to keep as close as possible to Jesus each day.

That prayer probably mentioned certain *facts* about the relationship with Him. And that's vital! If you don't remind yourself of these facts every day, what you say to Him is going to depend far too much on fluctuating moods. In some moods, praying is about the last thing you feel like doing.

In case you'd like to borrow any of it, a 'facts prayer' is printed overleaf. I know you'll keep the content flexible (according to circumstances) and that you'll increasingly express thoughts from here in a way which makes them your own.

It won't be all talking, of course. Jesus will give you a *very* clear awareness about certain things if you 'listen'.

Always use this fact-based contact with your Friend (however you may be feeling). It has tremendous results. He gradually becomes so real to you that, wherever you are, whatever you're doing, you just take His presence for granted!

Lord, I thank You for these facts:
- *Thank You that you chose me.*
- *Thank You that I belong to You – always.*
- *Thank You that I have the greatest of life gifts – Yourself!*
- *Thank You for Your care through my life so far – providing for me, protecting me (often without my realising it).*
- *Thank you for all that You have 'sent' or 'permitted' in my life – because You have made it all harmonise with Your good purposes.*
- *Thank You for all my present blessings.*
- *Thank You for a growing experience of your very wonderful love.*

Here are more outlines of other suggested prayers – no need for them to be used all at once!

Lord, I'm sorry:
- *Sorry for the many times I've failed You.*
- *Sorry that I've not always used strength which would have enabled me to do so much better.*
- *Sorry for wrong tendencies in me which I have been slow to reverse, with Your help.*
- *Sorry for everything that has hurt your love – and Your expectations of me.*
  Please forgive me.

Lord, may Your will be done:
- *I trust You to over-rule any initiatives of mine which are contrary to Your will – and to add Your blessing to those things which are pleasing to You.*
- *I surrender myself completely to You, this and every day, so that what You want may happen in my life.*
- *Let me see Your will more and more clearly – so that I don't 'slow down' its working out.*
- *Thank You that Your wisdom is being carried out in my present circumstances.*

Lord, please help:
- *Those who are very frightened.*
- *Those who are broken-hearted, and see no purpose in living.*
- *Those who are unwanted.*
- *Those who are misunderstood.*
- *Those who have no food, shelter, security, in the world today.*
- *Those with no faith.*
- *My loved ones and others I now name before You.*
- *All those known to You who are in great need at this time.*
- *Please show me what I can do to best help those around me and*

to advance Your purposes.

Lord, I receive:
- Because I am united with You, and share Your life, I thank You for some more facts!
- I'm growing: in love, Your love;
- In peace, Your peace;
- In patience, Your patience;
- In wisdom, Your wisdom;
- In true joy, Your joy.

Lord, I thank You and praise You:
- For all that You are.
- For all that You have done for me (I owe everything to You).
- For all that You now mean to me.
- I praise You Lord Jesus, my Friend.
- I praise You, heavenly Father, so close to me in Jesus, my Lord.

Those needing help

In the 'Lord, please help' part, what is the most effective way to pray for someone we know to be in need? There are many approaches to this and, as you know, entire books have been devoted to the subject.

I'm sure that many of your own prayers for others will now be springing naturally from a growing trust in Jesus, our Lord, and from a growing concern about people around you. Because of this, they're likely to be answered prayers.

We should never prescribe for God what the person really needs (which is what we're often tempted to do) nor think that His response depends on our intensity, on any technique or on our flow of beautiful words.

By now, we're used to thinking about the love of Jesus, aren't we? Well, just imaginatively hold up the person who needs help in that love.

We noticed Susan at the office today. When we spoke to her, she was tense, on the verge of tears. She didn't want to say too much about the causes of what was bothering her – and what we said to her seemed so feeble and inadequate.

At the first opportunity we 'bring' Susan to Jesus, our Friend: 'Lord, please bless Susan. *You* know what's wrong. Please give to her what she really needs.'

And what should we be *wanting* for Susan? Above everything else, we should want her to experience the companionship of Jesus! As we pray for Susan, He may make us very aware of something more He wants *us* to do for her.

Don't forget that a prayer said *before* or *after* being with people is equally effective. For instance, if we know we're going to meet someone, the meeting should, ideally, fit into what the Lord is *already doing* about that encounter, because we've prayed!

Let's say we meet Andrew unexpectedly and try to say or do something helpful on the spur of the moment. The *important* thing is still the prayer we say about Andrew afterwards!

And, of course, you'll remember to *thank* Him during the days which follow for what He's doing in Andrew's life and for each person for whom you've prayed.

I'm pretty sure that prayer is no longer, for you, the frightening word it is for some. Prayer of any kind (as long as it isn't mechanical).

Any kind – praising, feeling ashamed, being grateful, being submissive, seeking guidance, concerned for other people. It's all making a very strong link between Jesus and you – a link which isn't going to break!

His gift

I'm sure you've noticed how much Jesus' peace is becoming part of you. You notice this when it's temporarily lost for some reason, don't you?

The sense of calm has grown if you've been 'with Him' a lot

– and sharing even the smallest details with Him.

Don't forget that Jesus wants you to have that peace, not just at certain periods, but uninterruptedly.

It's helpful, whenever you can, to make a short time for focusing on His peace. Something like this:

Dear Lord,
Even the thought of You brings peace. The thought of Your constant concern of me. The thought of how great You are. Your peace is a barrier against all that's harmful. And it's at work inside me, too.
Right now I rest in its influence.
May I carry Your peace with me.
May it pass to those I meet!
Thank you again.

Start of a Journey

We're almost at the end of our book, but only in the early stages of what's going to be an often – breathtaking journey – with Jesus.

There will be moments when you're tempted to think that it's all been a waste of time. Just resist that temptation, because you'll find that life shared with Jesus is *every bit as wonderful as described.*

His friendship won't clash with your human friendships – on the contrary, it's going to do such a lot for them.

Do you have a fairly solitary existence? His presence is going to bring you courage. It's going to give you something to hope for. It's going to bring a sense of not being alone for a single moment.

This is a good time to ask Him to make you aware of anything upon which you should be concentrating right now.

If you've found the book helpful, I'm glad! I'll be delighted if you now make the suggestions for times of quiet (and other parts you've found helpful) part of your way of life.

By now you've realised that you don't have to keep a lot of rules in order to hold on to Jesus, but here are some reminders of things which (from your side) will help to *deepen* the friendship. I'm sure that some have already become automatic.

Here they are:

- Offering each day to Him. Thank Him that He's going to bless and use the day – and He will.
- Ignoring Adrian and creating brief times in which to do nothing except to think of Jesus – and to take in all that He has to share.
- Thanking Him, often, for what He's doing (even in the absence of anything tangible).
- Making a regular time to look at Him in action in the Bible and to let His words shape the way you live. Taking a good look at God's *promises* in the Bible and applying them to *you*.
- Remember that, as you let in God's word in this way, you're letting in Himself!
- A word or just a look of *trust* – even when busy.
- *Noticing* the needs of people around you – and letting His love reach them through you.
- Seeing temptations which hit you, not as things to be 'struggled against', but as things to be despised!
- Asking His help for those *He* knows to be in great need of that help – at the time you're praying. You can be sure that He's making use of that prayer – usually for people you're never likely to meet!
- Sharing the hopes and the problems of others who are learning to know Jesus. It's still a world which largely ignores Him and He wants those like you who *are* interested to be together – a real part of Himself. So don't be afraid to get really involved in a church!
- Telling Him, from time to time, of your love and your trust

(however imperfect you still consider them to be). You're going to be among that minority who make God glad – by loving Him *for His own sake*. 'Ministering' to Him!

There will be days when you can't carve out as much time as you'd like to be 'with Him'. Don't worry, you can take it for granted that He's constantly thinking of all that concerns you!

Finally

On this journey with Jesus I know you won't be surprised if there are some tremendous conflicts, all sorts of problems (some of a type never encountered before) and, inevitably, some very sad times.

But I also know that you'll be keeping firmly in your mind that you have precisely the same Friend who has meant everything to the great saints throughout history.

Do you know something?

It means everything to Jesus that you're part of Him. And it means everything to Him that you're on His side.

The friendship of Jesus is yours. Your Friend wants you to *use* Him, increasingly.

He's actually living in you – so don't waste Him, will you?

He is *enjoying* you!

Jesus says: 'Live in Me – and I in you.'

Dear Lord,

I believe that what now exists between us is going to last for ever. I know that things won't always be easy – but I have You, the Saviour of the world, as my companion. I trust completely in all You are and I look forward to what I can become, united with You! For the remainder of my life I want to share every experience with You. In the working out of Your plan for this world. You can count on me.

His promise: 'I am with you – always.'

God's Secret

Contents

Introduction

There is a secret which God wishes to share!

Many have found the secret and it has revolutionised their way of living. Without the discovery, a Christian's life may not be as victorious as it is meant to be.

Here is a typical cry-from-the-heart. I wonder how many would identify with it?

I do have occasional bursts of warm faith. I can appear joyful and very 'spiritual' at times. But I wonder how much I really have changed since I became a believer?

And could this be the desperate prayer which we may find ourselves saying?

Lord, I am so busy on Your behalf; I say all the right things to others about knowing You and trusting You. I know that I would be a much worse person without You … but I can't hide from You that there is so much darkness, so much sheer doubt, so many failure-areas …

There are lots of hurt places which still need Your healing. I can't go on excusing periods of coldness and doubt by saying that it's 'normal'.

Lord, You must know that I'm not a minute-by-minute Christian …

There's often pressure upon Christians to present a 'joyful', 'victorious' image. I have met many who have done this for a while, refusing to admit to any doubts or difficulties, but then have broken down – sometimes tearfully – in my presence.

That's why we must never be afraid to confront ourselves fearlessly, ready to admit that, inside, there is often a huge vacuum! If we want to learn God's secret, realism is always the best starting-place for learning it.

Chapter One

I wonder whether we could imagine ourselves, standing, completely alone, under the night sky? ...

For a few moments, we have broken free from all our usual supports and friendships. We haven't got with us those well-loved books of devotion or even the memories of them. It is silent and chill. I wonder if the darkness echoed, just a little, inside us?

Do we have, not so much a sense of God, but a sense of longing?

For some of us, in spite of our surface 'assurance', there may even have been moments of not wanting to go on living.

We may find those star-systems, glimpsed through the clouds, very attractive, but so ... indifferent.

And God? Well, perhaps we thought that we had it all nearly tied down, but, as we stand here in the darkness, there is a feeling that God is only our own self-comforting invention?

Isn't the uncomfortable truth that we're absolutely alone?

And in so, in the silence, we seem unable to rely on all the uplifting things which others have written. We remember, rather uncomfortably, how we have reassured other people with faith-filled phrases, which sounded a little hollow to ourselves!

Dare we trust any longer those warm faith-evocative occasions when we 'praised' God, along with other Christians? Dare we look at existence courageously – even if the conclusion could be the agnosticism which we have pitied in others?

Can what is all around us here in the darkness have any possible interest in us?

Whatever has happened to the super-structure of faith and confidence which we thought we had acquired?

Does the pain of life which we observe every day, fit best into a universe which is dark and uncaring?

We linger for a little longer and, feeling empty, leave our little spot under the stars.

Soon, though, we will return ...

A few days later we find ourselves out under the stars once more. On that previous occasion, there was the strange feeling that the emptiness was, paradoxically, a somewhat mystical experience. But we're quite prepared, now, for another cold 'moment of truth'. Here, in the darkness, the old doubts come rushing back.

But it's not very long before there's a sense of something happening as part of this vacuum-experience. It's almost as if the darkness is trying to get through to us.

It's as if existence is enfolding us and making us feel very secure, even in the absence of tangible sources of security.

We daren't tear ourselves away, because it seems that something is being whispered into our hearts, ever so gently:

My child, this universe which you are pondering is Myself ... I am expressed in it I share both the light and the sadness of your life – and the lives of all My children.

Suddenly, the darkness has become a caring environment, as the heart-whisper continues:

My child, I have made this creation the setting in which you can find true knowledge of Me ... The dark places are the very places where you can make the blinding discovery of My love ...

It is a love of which this universe is merely on partial expression ...

This incredible universe is not so much based on creative power, but an expression of love! We're sure that we have come across this description many times previously, but now, it fills our thoughts.

We're desperate to learn more, feeling the sense of a secret about to be revealed.

Suddenly there is a strong feeling that we have to give a name to the presence enfolding us here in the darkness. A word keeps intruding – a very familiar word, but this time causing us to feel a thrill.

The name which persists in coming to us is – 'Jesus'.

We begin to wonder how on earth people could ever regard that name as just the relatively narrow object of worship of one of the major world religions.

We find ourselves whispering the name with a sense of awe ... whispering it to ourselves – and to Him.

Our heart registers a response from the surrounding presence:

Yes, this is My universe, and because of Me, God is now knowable for you.

After a moment or two, we have the strongest possible impression of some very familiar words – though they never sounded quite like this before:

Come to Me ...

All at once, the daunting couldn't-care-less universe is eloquent and protective. This inescapable presence, under the night sky, must be the risen Saviour of our planet.

'Jesus' suddenly means Someone always existing – the place where love, suffering, doubt, the mysterious creation and the 'me' who has evolved through the centuries begin to come together and to make sense, at last.

Chapter Two

By now, there is no tearing oneself away from this encounter in the stillness. And soon, a further word is whispered into our heart:

My child, there is so little real knowledge of Me ...

So many who claim to know Me are, in reality, missing the way ...

Many subtle by-paths away from Me are not recognised for what they are ...

So many have become content with second-best, and feel that humanity cannot attain more in this life ...

Many have believed the lie that it is not possible really to know My presence consistently. And yet knowing Me is a gift which I have for any child of Mine.

When someone comes to know Me, that person may be mistrusted, or seen as deserving of pity.

So many cannot accept, fully, the truth revealed about Myself, and cannot accept My power to change lives.

Many who bear My name may be virtually blind about what, in the name of 'religion', can be pathetic hindrances to knowing Me ...

Well! Here, under the night sky, we're not conscious of feeling cold or alone any more. There is now the even more persistent feeling that we're going to learn something crucial, a God-given secret, which will somehow change us.

Even now, we realise that we are not as confused as we used to be. We realise that something deeper than merely new insight is being given to us. There's a strong feeling that, when we go among people again, we'll never forget what is being shown to us. We feel that never again will we believe those who claim that it's impossible to say 'I know'. We'll never again be content with that second-best.

Why didn't we realise, earlier, that God wants individuals to experience His protective and tenderly-loving nature? We see, vividly, that any branch of religion which does not uncompromisingly lead to this, is sadly lacking.

These thoughts are confirmed by another whisper into our heart:

My child, I want you to come, as a pilgrim, on to the narrow way where My love can be found ...

So many hearts wish, desperately, to know that love ...

The most exciting journey you can make is to discover, in this life, the love of which I have spoken ... the love which lies behind this creation ...

The world continues to feel a more secure place for a few wonderful moments. But we must face the fact that, in a world like this, doubt is sure to re-assert itself. What can we do to keep the sense of 'I know'?

We now feel the need to be fully concentrated because we sense that God is about to reveal something important.

Then, as we give Him our full attention, it gently comes:

My child, I want you to see that My love for you is not just an attitude; it is an influence.

Chapter Three

So that's it. An influence ...

Well! We have to admit that this seems a rather low-key divine secret! But this low-key secret is, in fact, a crucial one.

Here is God wanting us to know that He's not merely thinking of us lovingly, and occasionally intervening with a burst of power on our behalf. (Isn't that, honestly, what most of us feel?)

No. The truth being shown is a revolutionary one for us. God's love is, in fact, a change-bringing influence (there all the time), a conquering influence.

God's love is a power which reaches those deep places of the mind which are usually closed to us; it is something to affect every aspect of our existence. If we will let it!

Not an attitude, but an influence ...

So many Christians wish, desperately, to feel God's love more warmly, or to know that they really have changed from the people they were. For such people, God offers the discovery of a wonderful way through. He wants us to be receivers of His influence – rather like being tuned in to a TV or radio signal – if that isn't too homely an illustration!

As we learn to recognise God's constant love-influence, our lives, which are intrinsically ones of change and uncertainty, acquire a marvellous stability. This is because the influence is constant.

But just a moment, what about the barriers? Yes, the barriers existing in that very complex me, the barriers of temperament and those results of what life has done to me. How can the love-influence get past these?

And so, we throw this question back at God: 'What about the barriers?' After a moment or two, we suddenly realise that God didn't 'ordain' these barriers in order to make knowing Him a near-impossible process. The barriers may have been erected from our side – not all intentionally, of course – the result of life-experiences, reactions to pain, parental influences. But we now realise something else which is crucial about those barriers (and it's a wonderful realisation): God doesn't see them!

Oh, but surely those barriers are real?

The absence of love in my past, making it hard for me to relate, closely, to people (and to God, of course); the free-floating anxiety which attaches itself to almost everything; the sense of rejection; the sense of injustice, perhaps, about the way life has treated me, compared with others.

And then, there could be the barrier of a cold barren existence left after the death of someone greatly loved. Surely, all of these are tremendous obstacles to knowing God warmly and to enjoying His love?

But the message persists: God doesn't see these things as barriers against Himself. Painful areas (God would agree), but barriers? Emphatically, no.

Let us recognise those life-experiences, those temperament-limitations which we feel prevent us from experiencing God's love ... Then, a deep breath, as we imaginatively allow God to look right through all those barriers – a look of love right into the very deepest part of us.

However 'hopeless' we may have felt our circumstances or our personal makeup to have been, we start to see that God's love now has the power to pierce our defences.

I cannot emphasise too strongly that nothing can stop His love reaching us, nor our realising that love – simply because that love is conquering influence. Our supposed barriers can be cut down to size, at last.

And so, in the best tradition of the let's-start-today books, shall we begin, now, to look at ourselves in God's way, rather than as 'difficult subjects'? It may take a little courage, but let's say about those barriers: 'They may have seemed barriers to me – but they're not barriers to Him.'

Here is a prayer which we may like to use:

Dear Lord,
For so long I have seen all those weaknesses and life-experiences
as me. I see that these intruders can no longer stand in the way of
a wonderful relationship between us – one which You have always
wanted for me.
Right now, I concentrate upon Your love's influence, the divine
power which is beginning to change me – change me from someone
who wistfully tries to believe that I am a new person (or tries to
convince others that I am). Instead, under Your love's influence, I
am going to be that new person.
Thank You.

Chapter Four

If we peep in, imaginatively, at those encounters which Jesus our Lord had when He walked about on this planet, we'll see the love-influence at work.

And we'll notice something disappearing from those whom Jesus met – their past.

People like Zaccheus (away went his greedy past), Mary Magdalene (away went her promiscuous way of life), Bartimeus (an end to his shut-in world) ...

Hundreds of ordinary people finding that the love which flowed from Jesus meant the past dropping away like a dead weight.

So much so, that those people reacted joyfully far beyond mere gratitude, didn't they? They knew that something wonderful had happened to them. The past, with its barriers to happiness, had been left behind – for good. The look from Jesus had been more than a look of compassion or understanding; it had been a look of power.

People were changed by the influence of love coming from Him – in many cases without specific prayer or word of command.

But surely, some may be thinking, surely we can't all expect the same instant changes?

I agree. A book which glibly suggested this, would raise false hopes, wouldn't it?

Yes, of course it's wonderful if we're suddenly set free from the past in dramatic fashion. But what really matters is that there is now to be a very definite improvement – and this is precisely what consciously being in the divine influence will bring about. Often more quickly than we dreamt was possible!

When we find God's secret and see His love for us as a decisive influence, change must begin.

It can be very helpful to picture God's love-influence as a light, powerfully affecting every part of us. We can picture Jesus, the source of that divine influence, His arms outstretched towards us, giving to us ...

This powerful love-influence acts in two ways: firstly, upon all that is in us, making us tranquil – both about the present and the future; secondly, upon our relationships, and all that involves the world around us.

We now notice how the divine influence brings results where intense effort has failed.

We're opening the door to a completely new life. The Saviour of the world, the source of power, is now central to us.

Don't worry if some situations 'appear' unchanged – for a time at any rate. Just resolutely thank the Lord that changes are happening.

Unless we are, perhaps, a weary book-reviewer who may be irritated by reputation, don't see the chapters of this book as needing to be 'got through'. Allow lots of time between the chapters for learning to recognise the love-influence at work – recognised as we start each day, and continuing until we sink into that same influence at bedtime.

Lord,

It's exciting to think that for the rest of my life I can be aware of the active influence of Your love upon me. Right now I will begin to live consciously in the light of that influence.

I know that as I recognise the power contained within Your love, so much will be changing. As I do so, I will see clearly, at last, what really is important; I will see those disturbing factors in their true proportion. Thank You again, Lord, for the changes which You are starting to bring about.

Chapter Five

What is the use of a future if it is merely a continuation of what exists now?

Until now, we may have felt that our past must, inevitably, reach into the future and ruin it, even if we're still quite young!

We may cling, grimly, to Jesus' promise of a bright future after tribulation, but 'realism' keeps intruding: 'Here I am, stuck with this personality and its fears, destined to grow older in a difficult world.'

Resignation to the years ahead for many of us.

But God has let us into His secret!

Accepting the power of God's love-influence, the past need not mould the future for one day longer.

We know, of course, that there will be challenges. The bodily machine will break down in various ways, the environment may become suddenly frightening, there will be loss of loved ones, and heartbreak.

In fact, there will be the strongest temptation to react to circumstances in the old ways, forgetting all about the love-influence. But even in the darkest places light will come if it has become second nature to live in that influence. In the darkness, that influence of Jesus will beam down upon us and give us strength just to hold on, though heartbroken at times.

An experiment. Try to think simultaneously about (a) that uncertain future, with its potential for great difficulty and (b) Jesus' love in that future.

How does the future seem as we do this?

Normally, (b) starts to dissolve the apprehension contained in (a).

What the love-influence of God does, in fact, is to light up the future and transform so much of our natural apprehension.

Obviously, some questions that must be asked: Will we be able to keep our attention upon the love-influence in the midst of the very painful daily realities: the failing marriage, the financial problems, the difficult colleagues, the person who won't forgive us?

Certainly, these things could distract us, completely, from focusing upon God's influence. But do remember that these experiences must be classified (like all the other things we have mentioned) as barriers which do not exist, as such, for God. Therefore, we can see these things as unable to prevent God's influence from reaching us.

In case anyone thinks that what has been said is just playing with words, we have only to look at our Bible to see the acquired skill, possessed by so many of its heroes, of managing to be lost in God's love in the most awful human situations; they kept within the love-influence, even if they didn't always think of it, precisely, in this way!

Just look at some of the familiar hymns to see the transforming of dark circumstances by those who had learned the same secret.

One of those things which Jesus does so wonderfully is to assure us that He has already arrived at those places which cause us to be afraid, waiting for us with all that we need.

In the influence of Jesus' love, the future must, ultimately, be a bright one, because that influence represents power over everything which could now make us afraid.

Dear Lord,

For a little while I'm going to sit down and look at the future! I'm going to see that future in the light of Your love's powerful influence upon me.

You are well aware that my human nature shrinks from future illness or loneliness, but I know that when I reach those places, Your influence will still be there, helping me to be calm and courageous. Even in the darkest circumstances, I know that the influence of Your love will mean hope can never disappear.

Thank You.

Chapter Six

To use the phrase 'the light of God's love-influence' is not just a figure of speech. We really do see things with increased clarity as that light is turned upon the world around us.

The more we are open to the love-influence, the more we can evaluate what is in the complex pattern of events, and of people, of which we're part. We now have a light by which we can see beyond the superficial; we see, instinctively, what can't be trusted, we see that which it would be foolish to follow, that which represents danger. In the same way, we begin to see the sheer goodness in people who may present an exterior which we don't like very much!

And, of course, under the same light, we see more clearly what is in us. We will see more readily what is still coming between Jesus and ourselves.

Some of the baffling choices are now dealt with almost instinctively – people of an anxious temperament taking a little longer!

Decisions ... Perhaps there's a choice which we know, deep within us, is going to change the direction of our life. Instead of the usual list of 'for and against', with things delicately balanced, we must deliberately let the light of God's love-influence shine upon the problem.

As we learn to look at the situations of choice, very aware of the love-influence, there is a growing instinct about the right course. We gain the ability to see the situation through the eyes of Jesus, as His light falls upon it.

We find that it becomes second nature to test the situations into which we move by the light of the love-influence; we develop an alertness in 'interpreting' the signals which the world gives to us.

Under the influence of God's love, our own judgement is

starting to blend with His own wisdom.

There's no need to be afraid, once we've made a choice in the light of love's influence. Sometimes the things resulting immediately from the choice will cause us to panic or to have grave misgivings – 'Oh dear, what have I done?' But God does not deceive us; the long-term results of choosing by His light are always sure.

By the way, what an improvement there is in relationships when they are the subject of divine enlightenment! We have seen how evil constantly lies to us, how we can become paranoid, and feel that we have to defend ourselves against someone's ill-will towards us. Things which we have 'accepted' in our minds, from evil, can lead to a disastrous intention being formed.

'With Me, you won't be walking in the dark any more,' says Jesus, in that exciting teaching about Him being the light of the world. It's all about His love keeping us on a safe path in a confusing world, as we allow its influence.

Dear Lord,
I will remember, as a discipline, to look at every situation in the light of Your love's influence. I know that, as You enlighten me, I will avoid all sorts of things which would hold up my progress, or be disastrous for myself – and others.
Thank You.

Chapter Seven

Here's John; it's always a tricky moment when I'm face-to-face with him. John is one of those moody Christians ...

I'm sure that John doesn't feel the slightest warmth towards me, or approval of me. I could dodge this encounter by walking neatly to the right, as if I hadn't seen John; at least I'd be spared my resentment if he responded to my 'hello' with a cold parting of the lips.

But here I am, temporarily forgetting the love-influence!

Remembering the divine influence, I find the courage to look at John straight in the eyes, and greet him warmly.

Does John respond? If he doesn't, so what? The love-influence gave me a victory; it dissolved, in advance, my feeling of annoyance if John was as distant as ever. As I focus upon the divine influence, we can't rule out John being 'melted' and responding warmly.

In any event, I'll always say a little prayer for the Lord to bless John, who may have great needs.

One of the obvious aspects of focusing upon the love-influence of Jesus is that of being able to rise above previous reactions to the way in which others treat us.

Not being robots, we're going to react with a degree of sensitivity to people around us, but as we learn to use the love-influence, it can envelop the hurts and then dissolve them.

It's as if Jesus is saying 'Now, come on. Are you brooding on what that person said to you? Are you brooding on how that other person gossiped about your character? Are you forgetting to think of My love-influence?'

How often we forget to contrast the impermanence of the world's circumstances with the ongoing nature of Jesus' love. The great saints always stressed how everything is passing except God. But sadly we often forget this.

As we learn the skill of letting the love-influence dissolve hurts, we realise that we really have moved on to a higher plane! The presence of the Source of the love-influence becomes stronger and far more important than the fortunes and misfortunes of each day, and we gain a wise detachment about these things. Life's passing experiences are transformed by the permanent fact of Jesus, so that His love-influence becomes the background against which everything else is seen, wonderfully strengthening our relationship with Him.

St Paul stressed that love goes on for ever. And so, therefore, does its influence!

Lord,

I let the light of Your love-influence shine upon those painful areas which are due to other people's imperfections and to my own. I think of those things now, slowly, one by one; I think of the people with whom there may exist a state of disharmony. I allow the influence of Your love to dissolve all resentment.

The power of Your love is helping me to see things in their true proportions at last; I see Your love making these disturbances powerless to affect the upwards direction of my walk with You.

Thank You.

Chapter Eight

We would all like to be free – from something, or, perhaps, from someone! I have to smile, when listening to some of the 'pop' songs at how often we get the phrase 'Set me free' – or, as one unfortunate romantic partner was told: 'Get out of my life!'

If we could eliminate every troublesome relationship from our life we would still want to be free from things within us, wouldn't we? Many people who fiercely claim to be free and independent (especially of those oppressive religious beliefs!) are shaped by their environment much more than they realise.

Of all the things from which people would like to be free, I'm sure that fear would be near the top of the list. About fear, we must remember that Jesus once said, 'If I set you free, you really are free!' What a promise! We soon find that one most important aspect of the love-influence is that it is liberating.

Fear is typical of the human problems upon which the influence of Jesus has a transforming effect, succeeding where 'positive-thinking' methods fail. When Jesus begins to set us free, it opens the way for a heightened experience of life's many good things, which fear (in one form or another) usually manages to spoil.

When the power contained in the love-influence loosens some of the chains from the past, it's as if we can begin to be a little more adventurous. We're given permission to live!

I mentioned fear because it is the favourite weapon of those supernatural evil forces which oppose God's loving plans for us. (I haven't referred to those evil forces so far, but can assure any sceptical person that it is not old-fashioned to take these forces seriously. Jesus did – and does!)

Fear drives us into chaotic situations, into hatreds, into assassinations, into world wars, and into self-destruction. Fear makes us morbidly concerned about what people think of us, it warps our judgements and it freezes the love which we could feel for people.

Our various fears do diminish as we very deliberately open ourselves up to the influence of Jesus' love. This I can promise.

Most of us are aware of another sinister area which is tangled up with fear – that is, of course, the self-condemning part of us. I am not talking about the healthy disgust with ourselves when we have behaved badly. I mean the nagging 'neurotic' guilt which so often persists even when we have asked God for forgiveness, and honestly believe that we have received it.

Again, nagging guilt can be a favourite weapon of evil forces; if evil can make us accept the lie that we don't deserve forgiveness, then we may become permanently self-condemned. It is vital to use the love-influence to wear down these areas of guilt. We must be very bold when receiving the Lord's forgiveness. We must look into the light of His love and say 'Thank You, Lord. I have nothing for which to condemn or to punish myself.' We need to do this every time, so that it really sinks down. We need to say it very defiantly to evil too: 'The Lord has forgiven me. There is nothing for which to condemn or to punish myself.'

Those greatly used by God soon find that evil is both subtle and powerful. We must, therefore, keep firmly in mind that the love-influence is a power, a power greater than those opposing forces, a power possessed only by the Creator of the universe.

The roots of fear and self-condemnation may lie very deep but they are loosened by that power as we surrender to it. Love setting us free.

Lord,
I believe that unless it comes from You, freedom is partial and temporary. With all my heart I accept Your promise of freedom. I realise that the influence of Your love is a liberating influence.
Thank You.

Chapter Nine

A very short chapter, just to remind us that, as Jesus sets us free, it is in order to take us somewhere else!

Remember, always, those outstretched hands. Jesus does not set us free to live in a vacuum, but in order to make sure that we are lifted into His Kingdom of love – permanently.

Yes, Jesus has a great longing. From our birth He longs to draw us into Himself, into eventual oneness. If we live in the love-influence that is precisely what is happening.

We must be quite clear that we're not being brought into a comfortable trouble-free existence, escaping from earth's more painful places; that is not promised to us. But the road upon which the love-influence shines (though not trouble-free) is the only truly safe road.

Although we have to live to the world's timetable, to a large extent, we can look into that love-influence and be immersed in another dimension within seconds. All this can be combined with the simplest whisper of a phrase such as 'In Your love'.

Just as times of prayer and Bible-reading are crucial, so are those recollections of His love-influence which always mean that the ever-present Lord Jesus lifts up our thoughts to where they belong!

Dear Lord,
Help me to see Your influence each day as my true and permanent environment.
Thank You.

Chapter Ten

Already, many will have noticed a very important aspect of the divine love-influence – its power to heal.

Initially the influence would have been a cleansing one – the light of God burning up all sorts of wrong ways of thinking.

Cynicism, intolerance, grudges, begin to feel increasingly uncomfortable guests in us, and prepare to leave.

We find ourselves taking sides with God against things in us which we had tolerated – sometimes almost affectionately! It is all part of healing.

Without even asking, specifically, for healing in a particular area, the consciousness of the divine influence is, in itself, a healing consciousness.

We need to be quite specific about what is happening as the love-influence reaches us, and deliberately to thank God for it – 'Thank You, Lord, for the healing of Your love'. This is no make-believe process, no mere 'self-conditioning' regime, but simply allowing the power of the Creator at work. The healing of God's love-influence is especially true in the sphere of the emotions. Emotional healing, of course, can so often affect, beneficially, the physical.

I do realise that many have been to healing services, had hands laid on them, perhaps, but are not conscious of 'being healed'. Many are tempted to abandon their faith. For anyone in this category I would say, 'Don't stop fully opening yourself up to the love-influence every day – even after many disappointments about specific requests.' This influence just cannot help in some way bringing about good results, even if, for the moment, it isn't the specific need uppermost in our minds.

Many things promise to 'renew' us; some of them do for a time, but are limited. The love-influence of Jesus, however, is the one miraculous renewing force, making new the essential you and me – the spirit, which is so dear to God.

Almost every writer on healing today will tell us that it is a subject far wider and more intricate than we could imagine. But we can be very sure always of the healing nature of Jesus' love. There's not true healing outside it.

We can, therefore, thank Him for all that is within us which His love's influence is healing, from the very moment that we opened ourselves up to it.

Dear Lord,
As Your love-influence reaches me, thank You that so many aspects of my existence are being renewed. Thank You that physically, emotionally and spiritually, there is, every day, a healing process. I shall go on looking towards You, and away from all those limitations!
Thank You.

Chapter Eleven

By this time we may be picturing, instinctively, the outstretched hands of Jesus, as His love-influence reaches us. One aspect of this reaching out is His supply.

Love guarantees supply. Nothing which Jesus sees as good for us now, or in the future, will ever be held back from us. The supply will be there for us precisely when needed – not before it is needed, and not, of course, when it's too late.

Those who have allowed Jesus to become their friend soon notice His anticipation. We ourselves can show anticipatory love to one another, but we only see its perfection in the way in which Jesus our Lord deals with us. If we allow His love's influence, Jesus is able to exercise this anticipatory supply in wonderful ways. We find needs met in a way which shows that He has been at work before we reached the need-situation.

The supply which comes from Jesus is without imperfection and is very much part of the love-influence; all it needs is our recognition. This is why anticipatory thanks are such a good idea: 'Lord, I don't quite see how I'm going to struggle through that occasion, but thank You that You will give me what I need.' 'Lord, it's beyond me to see how the bills will be paid, but thank You that You won't let me down,' and so on.

We find that the divine provision is by no means restricted to our material needs. The supply always comes in the form of very specific intervention – courage given at that interview, patience given in a demanding relationship, love given when nursing a sick person. Under love's influence, the spirit's needs are met in a way which the world can't possibly meet them. Jesus' awareness of our needs accounts for the many instances of the uncanny finding of lost articles when we've stopped looking frantically and prayed instead!

As living within the love-influence becomes second nature,

we can know that our spiritual, mental and material needs are being met. It all comes down to recognition. Recognition and thanks – both for the love-influence, and for the supply which always comes with it.

Lord,
Help me to develop the awareness of felt needs being met by Your unfailing supply. Even when I don't recognise a need, or when I forget to call on You, I know that Your supply will be there for me. Thank You.

Chapter Twelve

Let us keep that picture of Jesus reaching out to us for a few moments. Not only is He meeting needs, but reaching out to put something of His own nature into us. Yes, the love-influence means absorbing what He is.

Already, because God made us in His own likeness, there are reflections, in us, of the divine qualities. Sadly, as we know, these reflections can become obscured. Jesus wants to reach into us and develop those divine qualities which we'll need for eternity!

Therefore, when we look up into that love-influence, it's really a look of agreement with all that He wants to do in us. We're giving our consent to the life of Jesus expanding in us.

We soon learn that our own efforts to shape our character are not enough. As St Paul found, it just has to be God's work – producing what mere attempts at self-improvement could never achieve.

It's quite possible for that rather apologetic person with a poor self-image to be a victorious person in the things which really matter. As we absorb the divine influence, we are bound to be winning all sorts of victories – not always recognised at the time.

The qualities we have absorbed start to be available for other people. This is the often-forgotten way (more than words) which draws others to Him.

Just think of what we're absorbing!

Or, better still, who we're absorbing.

The usual warning has to be given, of course. We don't peer anxiously to see if we're becoming reflections of Jesus! We simply allow the absorption-process and keep our gaze upon the Source.

I realise that the concept of Jesus at work in us, making us more like Himself, is hardly original! But what may be new for many of us – and decisive – is discovering the wonderful interior-changes which come from living, consciously, within that influence.

Lord,
I need to be much more like You in order to negotiate this present existence vicariously. Let me look into Your constant influence of love; let this be my consent to Your work in me, as I absorb Your qualities.
Thank you.

Chapter Thirteen

Jesus expanding His influence, not only in us, but through us ...

'Serving God'. Oh dear, this is so often represented as an up-hill occupation – something which we may need to force ourselves to do, bringing just occasional satisfaction.

There is a far better way of looking at what we do for God. As we focus upon the love-influence, it means that we're living in the light; we then realise that we have an opportunity to let other people live in that same light! We're now in the best possible state to respond to the world and its needs.

Here is Mary, who seems to be in a shocking state when we bump into her. We don't need to think of our 'serving' or 'helping' Mary. Better to picture the light of the divine love-influence shining on both of us, and then let our conversation take place within that light.

Of course, we wouldn't embarrass Mary by telling her that we were both within the love-influence of Jesus at that moment!

But, for our part, we would listen to what Mary has to say, firmly believing that His light, His influence, is all around us, as He gives us the right words.

Visualizing Jesus' love-influence is very relaxing when encountering others. It goes far beyond playing at make-believe and making nice, mental, 'spiritual' pictures; the Lord Jesus is right there – guiding our conversation, prompting us about what we might do for someone. Although she may not realise it, Mary is a receiver of that powerful divine influence; she is sharing it with us at that moment, and it's the beginning of her need being met, if she is willing.

If we're learning the art of resting, consciously, in the love-influence when with others, this is the best possible condition for His power to flow. No need for a contrived setting, such as a praise-filled Christian convention, but simply letting the influence of love take over in that quiet one-to-one contact.

As we 'carry' the love-influence around with us, we must value every meeting we have – refusing impatience if a person is not the one we were hoping to see! In some way Jesus will be reaching out from us, even in the most casual-seeming or 'unresponsive' encounter.

To mention Mary yet again, the love-influence will be breaking down barriers in her. And if we find ourselves offering to pray with Mary, we can be absolutely sure that there, in the love-influence, a power to heal and uplift her is being released.

Normally, we can never be sure whether our 'words of wisdom' or attempts at persuasion are hitting any target. If we're forgetting the presence of Jesus, they could well be wasted efforts! If, however, we consciously keep within that influence of power, then everything occurring will have a lasting quality about it.

If we keep in the light of the love-influence I firmly believe that we are projecting it to those for whom we pray (as a fact, not just something within our own mind). Our prayer will be Spirit-led and there will be that wonderful assurance that someone is receiving, according to the need which God sees.

The process is completed by the word of thanks to our Lord, that either the prayer we said, or the contact we made, is being used, beyond any doubt.

As we realise that God's love is not merely an attitude towards us, but a powerful influence, we find one area of life after another being affected, including that of our sharing Him with others. God's Kingdom is one of light, and we're now helping to make it more widespread.

Dear Lord,
I will remember each day that, wherever I go, there is the influence of Your love. I will remember to see its light enfolding not only myself, but those whom I meet. I thank You, now, for all the good which will come from those encounters with others.

Chapter Fourteen

What about the unexpected crisis, when we wonder how on earth we can possibly come through, when we doubt our ability to deal with what has suddenly turned our life upside down?

Can the surrounding influence of the divine love make a difference? Can it make a difference, even when we've had the thought of not wanting to go on living?

We wouldn't be human if life's tragedies didn't have the power to shatter us. We only have to remember what happened when our Lord was called to the tomb of his friend, Lazarus. He did not 'react positively' or with detachment. He cried, didn't He?

One aspect of the vast subject of human suffering, which cannot be examined in depth here, is that the forces of evil work to exploit, and make much worse, the things which happen to us. It is because of this exploitation that we must, if we possibly can, allow the divine love to enter immediately that which has overwhelmed us. If we can do this, though still in a state of shock, terrible shock, we can be sure that Jesus' love now stands guard against those forces which would worsen the situation. All that we may be able to say with a broken voice is 'Lord, I trust Your love,' (even though the darkness ahead seems unrelieved).

As we make this almost helpless surrender to His love's influence upon our situation we may catch His whisper into our heart: 'My child, as I share this with you, let the power of My love help you to bear it.'

As we find just a little courage (very fragile) we realise that the influence of our Lord's love is mysteriously saving us from being completely broken.

Dear Lord,
I believe that You are able to share the darkest places – those major situations of fear which I feel I could never face, as I let Your love's influence enfold me.

Chapter Fifteen

Living consciously within Jesus' love-influence is all about contrast. Instead of those half-convincing statements about being a new person as a Christian, we now find that life in His love really does contrast sharply with life previously.

We can now confront the sort of daily situations in which we were usually defeated, and, in the light of His love, re-enter those areas victoriously.

Surrounded by His light, we face the circumstances with a power which we never dreamt we possessed.

We can reflect: 'Just to think that I could have been victorious in this sort of thing all along – instead of having those crushing failures.' The love-influence will produce contrasts such as these, if we really surrender ourselves to it:

Indecision giving way to boldness,

Agitation giving way to serenity,

Weakness giving way to courage,

Cynicism giving way to tolerance,

Self-concern giving way to out-going love,

Impulsiveness giving way to patience,

Persistent anxiety giving way to quiet joy.

Keeping aware of Jesus' influence, we're also going to recognise those important turning points – times when our choices will have a long-term significance. In His light we will choose with wisdom and see through any deception by forces opposed to God. The divine influence will be keeping out all that would confuse our mental processes; we will stop brooding upon hurts, or supposed hurts, and be able to pray for those 'troublesome' people – really wishing good to come to them. Contrasts at last!

Now, just a word to any who may feel that picturing the love-influence is a little unreal or stretching our imagination too far.

Many times during a day, in order to keep up his or her spirits, a person may 'picture' a beloved relative or friend. If we believe that God is just as real as that loved one or friend, then it makes sense to think much about His love!

Seeing the light of that influence is much more than a merely subjective vision, because whenever Jesus is, there is light; evil forces, which we may never have dreamt existed, can't operate in that light.

This light is often seen as a wall of fire around Christians in countries where naked evil is practised.

Let us remember, too, that as we turn to the light of Jesus' love, it meets His longing in a world which, on the whole, doesn't make much room for Him.

There is so much that could be written about that event two thousand years ago when God stepped into our world. What we see, linking everything together, of course, is love ...

As millions have done, we can look at the Cross and see love surrendering all, love taking the world's guilt-burden, love triumphant when all seemed lost. It is this love, seen on the Cross, which continues its victorious work. If we say 'yes' to its influence upon us, we will experience just how powerful is that love.

In this terribly unpredictable existence, the influence of Jesus' love is there to steady us, and we're no longer at the mercy of the rapidly changing fortunes of each day. We acquire the skill of avoiding things which we used to allow far too easily – simply because they were not illuminated!

Dear Lord,

Within the influence of Your love I can now act upon Your promise about making all things new. I will prove that new life in my changed reactions, because the power of Your influence will be there at every moment, for me to draw upon – producing contrasts with my past.

Chapter Sixteen

The most realistic way to see our future is to see it filled with Jesus. We must grasp God's eagerness for us to enjoy what He has been getting ready for us. The many promises of God are simply expressions of the love in which we now consciously live. If we look to love's brightness those promises will light up, too!

The walk within the love-influence is an upwards walk, and in a new direction. If we grasp Jesus by the hand, so to speak, He is lifting us forward – we will be lifted through those dark periods which may lie ahead.

As we remain in the influence of His love, Jesus our Lord will be removing all sorts of obstacles; these will include obstacles which we didn't pray about because we weren't aware of their existence! Jesus is our navigator. Keeping within His influence, we can be sure that He is excluding all that would be bad for our inheritance.

He will be making harmony of our circumstances. We need not run away from what lies ahead of us, because His light already shines on the road we've taken. The light says to us: 'Forget the past; the look is forward.'

As we become 'lost' in the love-influence shining upon our road, we realise that, eventually, there can only be better things in store for us – joys which will be permanent. Jesus becomes the hope of whatever particular existence is ours, expertly fitting the details into His plan for us; no evil forces will be able to frustrate that plan. Our destiny is perfection and not one step towards it will be taken alone. That perfection will be, essentially, all about love. Our growing love will blend with that divine love into which we look every day.

Obviously, within the light of Jesus' love, we won't be able to ignore the world's darkness – but we're going to see the light overcome the darkness. As we keep focused upon Jesus, we will learn to see His love as the background to all phenomena; we will see every problem against that background; we will see that all God's ways (including His justice) are, in fact, love-inspired.

The ever-growing sense of Jesus' love will draw out our worship of Him. Expressions such as 'dearest Lord', 'wonderful Lord' (which once seemed reserved for a spiritual elite, and well beyond us!) will now be spontaneous. Within the influence of His love we will find ourselves telling the Lord, gently, how much we love Him – in fact, just naturally having His name, frequently, on our lips. And we will often give Him that submissive look ('Whatever You wish, Lord').

Looking into the light of Jesus' love we'll be aware of a growing closeness which we can begin to use. We will very much have a sense of our walk being shared; we will know that we're loved even when, perhaps, human loves are missing. The influence coming from Jesus will be exerted to keep us on the road chosen for us. No longer will we think of heaven and earth as separate states, because our life here will have that definite heavenly dimension.

When events in our existence puzzle us from time to time, we'll remember God's knowledge of our future, and His certain influence in it; we will then be content to let Him work out His plans! If we allow it, the light of the love-influence will now burn steadily for us right through to the end of our life; it will be shining in us and around us, helping us to endure all that life can produce.

Where is the divine love-influence taking us? It is taking us to the place where love is everything.

As St Paul might have said in his famous letter to the Christians at Corinth: 'Love's influence achieves all things.'

Dear Lord,
Please make this a turning point. May there be a different quality of life as I surrender to the influence of Your love – whatever the circumstances. I know that I will see those circumstances transformed. Thank You.

OTHER BOOKS BY JOHN WOOLLEY

All the books below are "heart-whispers" from the
Risen Lord Jesus Christ to John Woolley, recorded by him

1. I Am With You
Tens of thousands all over the world have been helped
by this book in different ways. It seems to cover so many needs!
So many lives have been changed!

2. I Am With You For Young People
And The Young At Heart
"Heart-whispers" specially selected for the young

3. Abide In My Love
In this book we are taken into the mystery of suffering;
we look at the power of the Love which Jesus on the Cross
shares with the world's darkness. These words give courage and
offer a glimpse of eternity when all things WILL be made new

4. My Burden Is Light
Instructing us in the love of Jesus who shares all our lives
and our suffering and gives us hope, showing us
what a wonderful friend He is!

5. Many Mansions - Glimpses Of Heaven
Introducing us to Heaven where there is eternal
joy and happiness, telling us how all our tears will be
washed away in Jesus' presence

6. Mini booklets
Excerpts from the 5 books above are available
in booklet form - I Am With You, I Am With You For Young People
And The Young At Heart, Abide In My Love, My Burden Is Light, Many

Mansions, For Those Who Are Hurting,
You Are Never Alone.
These can be obtained FREE from "https://maps.google.com/
?q=2+Lauradale+Road+London+N2+9LU&entry=gmail&source=g"
2 Lauradale Road London N2 9LU, 020 8883 2665,
"mailto:contact@iamwithyou.co.uk" contact@iamwithyou.co.uk.

I AM WITH YOU FOUNDATION

Readers of John Woolley`s inspired words may join the
I Am With You Fellowship and there is no membership charge.
All in the Fellowship are remembered in prayer and are
encouraged to contact us about any need.
To join, please send your Christian name, surname, address
(including post code), phone no and email if available to:

I Am With You Foundation "https://maps.google.
com/?q=2+Lauradale+Road+London+N2&entry=gmail&source=g"

2 Lauradale Road London N2 020 8883 4736. website
"http://www.iamwthyou.co.uk/"www.iamwthyou.co.uk